COMING TO BE IS NOTHING BUT IMAGINATION

لوح الزمرد

حقٌّ لا شكَّ فيه صحيحٌ

إنَّ الأعْلى مِنَ الأسْفَلِ والأسْفَلُ مِنَ الأعْلى

عَمَلُ العَجائِبِ مِنْ واحِدٍ كما كانَتْ الأشياءُ كُلُّها مِنْ واحِدٍ بتَدْبيرِ واحِدٍ،

أبوهُ الشَّمْسُ، أُمُّهُ القَمَرُ،

حَمَلَتْهُ الرّيحُ في بَطْنِها،

غَذَّتْهُ الأرْضُ،

أبو الطَّلسَماتِ، خازِنُ العَجائِبِ، كامِلُ القوى،

نارٌ صارَتْ أرْضاً أعْزِلِ الأرْضَ مِنَ النّارِ،

اللّطيفُ أكْرَمُ مِنَ الغَليظِ،

بِرِفْقٍ وَحِكْمٍ يَصعَدُ مِنَ الأرْضِ إلى السَّماءِ وَيَنْزِلُ إلى الأرْضِ مِنَ السَّماءِ،

وَفيهِ قُوَّةُ الأعْلى والأسْفَلِ،

لِأنَّ مَعَهُ نورَ الأنْوارِ فَلِذلِكَ تَهْرُبُ مِنْهُ الظُّلْمَةُ،

قُوَّةُ القوى

يَغْلِبُ كُلَّ شَيءٍ لَطيفٍ، يَدْخُلُ في كُلِّ شَيءٍ غَليظٍ،

على تَكْوينِ العالَمِ الأكْبَرِ تَكَوَّنَ العَمَلُ،

فَهذا فَخْري وَلِذلِكَ سُمِّيتُ هِرمِس المُثَلَّثُ بِالحِكْمَةِ.

EMERALD TABLET

A Truth without doubt, wholly sound,
    that the highest is from the lowest
        and the lowest is from the highest.

The working of wonders is from the one,
    just as all things came from the one,
        by a single governance.

        Its father is the Sun and its mother is the Moon.
        The wind carries it in her belly.
        The Earth nourishes it.

Father of talismans,
    treasure-house of wonders,
        perfection of powers.

        Fire became earth.
        Separate the earth from the fire.
        The subtler is nobler than the gross.

With skilled work and restraint
    it will ascend from the Earth to Heaven
        and descend to Earth from Heaven.

And within itself is the power of the highest and of the lowest,
    within it is the light of lights,
        therefore darkness flees from it.

Power of powers.
    It can conquer every subtle thing,
        and penetrate everything gross.

Following the creation of the Macrocosm, the Work is completed.

This is my glory, and for that was Hermes named Thrice with Wisdom.

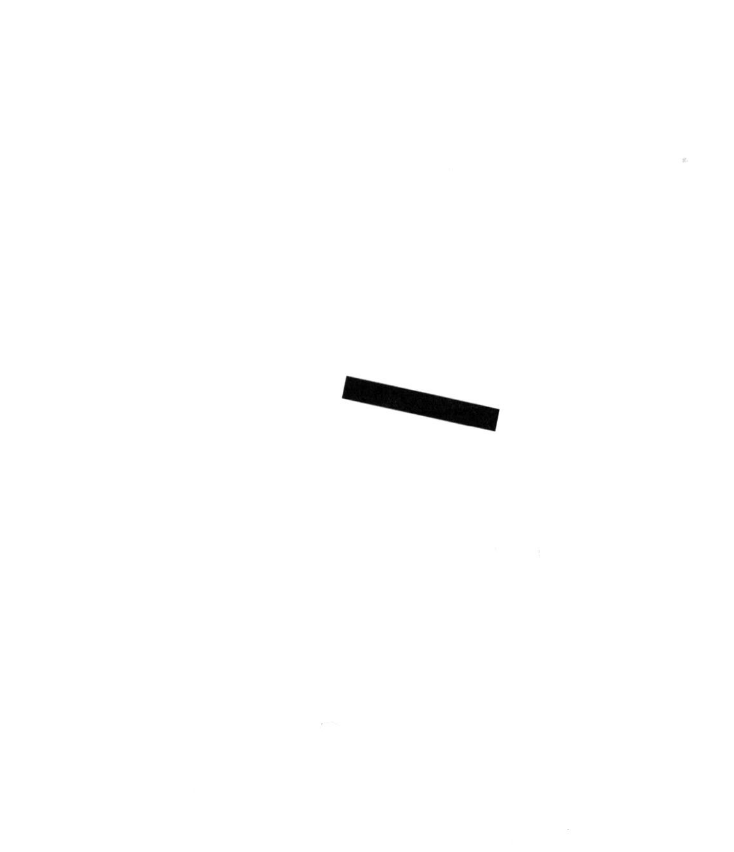

ALCHEMY THE POETRY OF MATTER

Brian Cotnoir

Book design, typesetting, and jacket design, by Lara Captan.
Hardcover glyph, illustrations, poems, and translations,
unless otherwise noted, by Brian Cotnoir.

Latin text is set in *Karmina* & *Karmina Sans* by TypeTogether.
Planet & Zodiac symbols and Greek text are set in the *Brill* typeface
by Tiro Typeworks.
The Arabic Emerald Tablet is set in *Falak* & *Kanat* by Lara Captan.

Opening quote *Corpus Hermeticum V.1*
End quote *Heraclitus frag.93 D-K*

ISBN 978-0-9993134-0-4

Printed in Canada

First Printing, 2017

Khepri Press
New York, NY
KhepriPress.com

Alchemy: The Poetry of Matter is also available as a limited edition hardcover as well as deluxe limited editions. For more information go to KhepriPress.com.

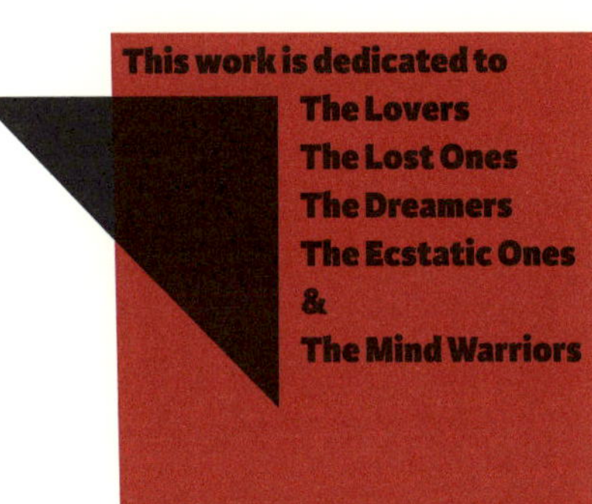
This work is dedicated to
The Lovers
The Lost Ones
The Dreamers
The Ecstatic Ones
&
The Mind Warriors

LIBER ENIM LIBRUM APERIT

One book opens another.

Rhasis

Ars Chemica Qvod Sit Licita Recte Exercentibus. 1566.
Book of Cratès. Trans. Adam McLean. Glasgow: Hermetic Research Series. 2002.
Chaldean Oracles. Trans. Ruth Majercik. Westbury: Promethean Trust. 2013.
Colour Index 3rd ed. Bradford, W. Yorkshire : Society. 1971.
The Way of the Pilgrim. Trans. Olga Savin. Boston: Shambala. 2001.
Picatrix. 2 Vols. Trans. from Arabic. Atallah and Holmquest. Seattle: Ouroboros. 2002–2008.
Picatrix. Trans. from Latin. Greer and Warnock. Adocentyn Press. 2011.
al-Hassan, Ahmad. *Islamic Technology.* London: Cambridge UP. 1986.
Agrippa, Henry Cornelieus. *The Three Books of Occult Philosophy.* Ed. Donald Tyson. Minnesota: Llewellyn Publications. 1998.
Alberti, Leon Battista. *On Painting.* Trans. John Spencer. New Haven: Yale UP. 1966.
Apollodoros. *Library 1.* 1.4. Trans. J.G. Frazer. Cambridge: Harvard UP. 1967.
Apollonius. *Kitāb Sirr al-Khalīqah wa Ṣan'at al-Ṭabī'a.* Ed. Ursula Weisser. Aleppo: University of Aleppo. 1979
Aquinas, Thomas and Joseph Rickaby S.J. *An Annotated Translation (With some Abridgement) of the Summa Contra Gentiles of Saint Thomas Aquinas.* London: Burns and Oates. 1905.
——. *Aurora Consurgens.* Trans. Marie Von Franz. New York: Bollingen. 1966.
——. *Aurora Consurgens.* Trans. Pasquale deLeo. Milano: Kemi. 2002.
Aristotle. *On The Heavens.* Trans. W.K.C. Gutherie. Cambridge: Harvard UP. 1953.
——. *De Generatione et Corruptione.* Trans. with notes C.J.F. Williams. Oxford: Clarendon Press. 1982.
——. *Meteorology.* Trans. H.D.P. Lee. Cambridge: Harvard UP. 1987.
——. *Metaphysics.* Trans. Richard Hope. Ann Arbor: University of Michigan Press. 1999.
——. *Physics.* Trans. Robin Waterfield. Oxford: Oxford UP. 1999.
Armstrong, Karen. *A History of God.* New York: Ballantine Books. 1994.
Ashmole, Elias. *Theatrum Chemicum Britannicum.* Hildesheim: Georg Olms Verlagsbuchhandlung. 1968.
Athanassakis, Apostolos and Benjamin Wolkow. *Orphic Hymns.* Baltimore: Johns Hopkins UP. 2013.
Bacon, Roger. *Opus Majus of Roger Bacon.* Trans. Robert Belle Burke. Philadelphia: University of Pennsylvania Press. 1928.

Bashier, Salman. *Ibn al-'Arabī's Barzakh*. Albany: SUNY Press. 2004.

Berthelot, M. *Les Origins de l'Alchimie*. Paris: Steinheil. 1885.

——. *Collection des ancien alchimistes grecs*. 4 vols. Paris: Steinheil. 1887.

——. *La Chimie au Moyen* Âge. Paris: Imprimerie Nationale. 1893.

Betz, Hans Dieter. *The Greek Magical Papyri in Translation*. Chicago: University of Chicago Press. 1996.

Bidez, J., *Catalogue des manuscrits alchimiques grecs*. Bruxelles: Lamertin. 1928.

Bobik, Joseph. *Aquinas on Matter and Form and the Elements*. Indianna: University of Notre Dame Press. 1998.

Boehme, Jacob. *The Signature of All Things*. Cambridge: James Clarke & Co. 1969.

Bonus, Petrus. *The New Pearl of Great Price*. New York: Arno. 1974.

Boyle, Robert. *The Work Diary of Robert Boyle*. 1647–1691.

——. *The Works of the Honourable Robert Boyle. Six Volumes. 1772.* Bristol: Thoemmes Press. 1999.

Brepohl, Erhard. *The Theory and Practice of Goldsmithing*. Trans. Charles Lewton-Brain. Portland: Brynmorgen Press. 2001.

Brouaut, Jean. *Traité de l'Eau de Vie ou Anatomie Théorique et Pratique du Vin*. Paris: Senlecque. 1646.

Browne, Charles Albert. *Papers Mss Col 418* New York City Public Library.

Bruno, Giordano. *On the Composition of Images, Signs, and Ideas*. Trans. Charles Doria. New York: Wills, Locker & Owens. 1991.

Brunschwig, Hieronymus. *Liber de arte distillandi de simplicibus*. Strassburg: Gruniger. 1500.

Burckhardt, Titus. *Alchemy: Science of the Cosmos, Science of the Soul*. London: Stuart & Watkins. 1967.

——. *Mystical Astrology According to ibn 'Arabī*. Louisville: Fons Vitae. 2001.

Burkert, Walter. *Homo Necans: The Anthropology of Ancient Greek Sacrificial Ritual and Myth*. Berkeley: University of California Press. 1983.

Caley, Earle Radcliffe. "The Leyden Papyrus X. An English Translation with Brief Notes." *J. Chem. Educ. Journal of Chemical Education* 3.10 (1926): 1149.

——. "The Stockholm Papyrus. An English Translation with Brief Notes." *J. Chem. Educ. Journal of Chemical Education* 4.8 (1927): 979.

Cicero. *The Republic*. Translated by Clinton Keyes. Cambridge: Harvard UP. 2006.

Cockren, Archibald. *Alchemy Rediscovered and Restored.* Philadelphia: David McKay Co. 1941.

Copenhaver, Brian P. *Hermetica: The Greek Corpus Hermeticum and the Latin Asclepius in a New English Translation, with Notes and Introduction*. Cambridge: Cambridge UP. 1992.

Corbin, Henri. *Creative Imagination in the Sufism of ibn 'Arabī*. Princeton: Bollingen. 1981.

——. *Alchimie comme arte hiératique*. Paris: L'Herne. 1986.

——. *Spiritual Body, Celestial Earth*. Princeton: Princeton UP. 1989.

Cotnoir, Brian. *Alchemy: A Weiser's Concise Guide.* Newburyport: Red Wheel Weiser. 2006.

——. *Emerald Tablet*. Trans. and commentary Brian Cotnoir. New York: Khepri Press. 2014.

——. *Dream: The Lunar Realm of Alchemy.* New York: Khepri Press. 2016.

——. *On the Animation of Statues*. New York: Khepri Press. 2016.

——. *On Alchemy and the Timing of Things*. New York: Khepri Press. 2017.

Crabb, George. *Universal Technological Dictionary. or Familiar Explanation of the Terms Used in All Arts and Sciences.* London: Baldwin and Cradock. 1833.

Crosland, Maurice. *Historical Studies in the Language of Chemistry*. Mineloa, NY: Dover Phoenix. 1978.

Dalai Lama. *Sleeping, Dreaming, and Dying*. Ed. F. Varela. Somerville: Wisdom Publications. 1997.

Dali, Salvator. *Conquest of the Irrational.* New York: Julian Levy. 1935.

Dawkins, Richard. *The Blind Watchmaker*. New York: Norton. 1996.

De Jong, H.M.E. *Michael Maier's Atalanta Fugiens.* Maine: Nicolas-Hays, Inc. 2002.

Descartes, René. *Discourse on Method and Meditations.* Indianapolis: Bobbs-Merrill. 1977.

DeVun, Leah. *Prophecy, Alchemy, and the End of the World*. New York: Columbia UP. 2009.

Dionysus Aeropagite. *Pseudo-Dionysus: The Complete Works*. Trans. Colm Luibheid and Paul Rorem. NJ: Paulist. 1987.

Dioscorides. *De Materia Medica.* Trans. Lily Y. Beck. Hildesheim: Olms-Weidmann. 2011.

Du Chesne, Joseph. *The Practise of Chymicall and Hermetical Physicke.* London: Thomas Creede. 1605.

Edgerton, S.Y. *The Renaissance Rediscovery of Linear Perspective*. New York: Basic Books. 1975.

Eliade, Mircea, and Willard Trask. *Yoga: Immortality and Freedom.* New York: Pantheon. 1958.

Eliade, Mircea. *The Forge and the Crucible*. Chicago: U of Chicago. 1978.

Faggin, Guiseppe. *Inni Orfici*. Rome: Asram Vidya. 2001.

Ficino, Marsilio. *Commentary on Plato's Symposium on Love*. Trans. Sears Jayne. Dallas: Spring Publications. 1985.

——. *Three Books on Life*. Trans. Carol Kaske and John Clark. New York: Medieval & Renaissance Texts. 1998.

Flamel, Nicolas. *His Exposition of the Hieroglyphicall Figures*. New York: Garland Publishing, Inc. 1994.

Florenskiĭ, P. A. *Iconostasis*. Crestwood, NY: St. Vladimir's Seminary. 2000.

——, Nicoletta Misler, and Wendy R. Salmond. *Beyond Vision: Essays on the Perception of Art*. London: Reaktion. 2002.

Forbes, Robert James. *Studies in Ancient Technology*. Leiden, Netherlands: E.J. Brill. 1964.

Fowden, Garth. *The Egyptian Hermes: A Historical Approach to the Late Pagan Mind*. Cambridge: Cambridge UP. 1986.

French, John. *The Art of Distillation*. London: Cotes. 1651.

Frick, Karl R. H. *Eröffnete Geheimnisse Des Steins Der Weisen: Oder, Schatzkammer Der Alchymie:*. Graz: Akadem. Druck- U. Verlagsanst. 1976.

Fück, J. W. "The Arabic Literature on Alchemy According to An-Nadīm (CE 987)." *Ambix* 4.3 (1951): 81-144.

Gagnon, Claude. *Description du Livre des Figures Hiéroglyphiques*. Montreal: Les Editions de l'Aurore. 1977.

Geber. *The Alchemical Works of Geber*. Trans. Richard Russel. Maine: Weiser. 1994.

Gentile, S., and Carlos Gilly. *Marsilio Ficino and the Return of Hermes Trismegistus*. Florence: Centro Di. 1999.

Glauber, Johannes Rudolph. *Des Teutschlandts Wohlfahrt Part IV*. Amsterdam: Jansson. 1656–61.

——. *The Works of Johannes Rudolph Glauber*. RAMS edition of Glauber's Prosperity of Germany Part 4. 1983.

Gombrich, E.H. *Symbolic Images*. Chicago: University of Chicago Press. 1985.

Goode, Jamie. *The Science of Wine: from vine to glass*. Berkely: University of California Press. 2005.

Guthrie, W.K.C. *Orpheus and Greek Religion*. Princeton: Princeton UP. 1993.

——. *A History of Greek philosophy. The Presocratic tradition from Parmenides to Democritus*. Cambridge: Cambridge University Press. 2000.

Hadot, Pierre. *Philosophy as a Way of Life*. Malden: Blackwell Publishing, Ltd. 1995.

Halleux, Robert. *Papyrus De Leyde: Papyrus De Stockholm Recettes.* Paris: Les Belles Lettres. 2002.

Haq, Sayed Nomunal. *Names, Natures and Things: the Alchemist Jābir ibn Hayyān and his Kitāb al-Aḥjār.* Dordecht. Kluwer Academic Publishers. 1994.

Heraclitus. *On the Universe.* Trans. Jones, W.H.S. Cambridge: Harvard. 1967.

Hesiod. *Hesiod: Vol. 1, Theogony, Works and Days. Testimonies.* Trans. Glenn W. Most. Cambridge: Harvard UP. 2006.

Hippocrates. *Hippocrates Collected Works I.* Trans. W. H. S. Jones. Cambridge: Harvard UP. 1984.

Holmyard, E.J. *Alchemy.* London: Penguin Books. 1957.

Homer. *Odyssey.* Trans. Robert Fitzgerald. New York: Doubleday. 1961.

Hopkins, Arthur John. *Alchemy, Child of Greek Philosophy.* New York: Columbia UP. 1934.

Iamblichus. *The Exhortation to Philosophy.* Trans. Thomas M. Johnson. Grand Rapids: Phanes Press. 1988.

——. *Theology of Arithmetic.* Trans. Robin Waterfield. Grand Rapids: Phanes Press. 1988.

——. *On the Pythagorean way of Life.* Trans. John Dillon, Jackson Hershbell. Atlanta: Scholars Press. 1991.

——. *De Anima.* Trans. Finamore and Dillon. Atlanta: Society of Biblical Literature. 2002.

——. *Iamblichus, De Mysteriis.* Trans. Emma C. Clarke, John M. Dillon, and Jackson P. Hershbell. Atlanta: Society of Biblical Literature. 2003.

Ibn al-'Arabī. *The Tarjumān al-Ashwāq.* Trans. Reynold A. Nicholson. London: Theosophical Publishing House. 1978.

——. *The Bezels of Wisdom.* Trans. R.W.J.Austin. Mahwah: Paulist Press. 1980.

——. *Meccan Revelations Vol. I, II.* Trans. Chodkiewicz, Chittick, Morris. New York: Pir Press. 2002–2004.

Ibn al-Haytham. *Optics.* Trans. A.I. Sabra. London: Warburg Institue. 1989.

Ibn Ḥayyān, Jābir. *Dix Traités d'alchimie.* Trans. Pierre Lory. Paris: Sinbad. 1983.

Ibn Sīna. *Liber Canonis Avicenne.* Trans. Arnald de Villanova. 1507.

——. *The Canon of Medicine Vol. I.* Laleh Bakhtiar and O. C. Gruner. Great Books of the Islamic World. 1999.

——. *The Canon of Medicine Vol. II.* Laleh Bakhtiar. Great Books of the Islamic World. 2012.

Ibn Umail, Muhammad. *Book of the Explanation of the Symbols. Kitāb Ḥall ar-Rumūz*. Theodor Abt and Wilfred Madelung eds. Zurich: Living Human Heritage Pub. 2003.

Ideler, Julius Ludwig. *Physici Et Medici Graeci Minores*. Berolini: Reimer. 1842.

Ignacius of Loyola. *The Spiritual Excercises of St. Ignatius.* Trans. Louis J. Puhl, S.J. New York: Random House. 2000.

Job of Edessa. *Book of Treasures*. Trans. A. Mignana. Cambridge: Heffer & Sons. 1935.

John of the Cross. *Dark Night of the Soul.* Trans. Miribai Starr. New York: Riverhead Books. 2003.

Kerenyi, Carl. *Dionysos: Archetypal Image of Indestructible Life.* Princeton: Princeton UP. 1976.

Klossowski de Rola, Stanislas. *The Golden Game*. New York: Thames and Hudson. 1996.

Kraus, Paul. *Jābir ibn Ḥayyān:* Contribution à l'histoire des idées scientifiques dans l'Islam, *Vol. I, II.* Natural Sciences in Islam, Vol. 67, 68. Frankfurt: Goethe University. 2002.

Kunckel, Johan. *Ars Vitraria Experimentalis.* Frankfurt and Leipzig. 1679.

LeBerge, Stephen. *Lucid Dreaming.* Los Angeles: Tarcher. 1985.

Lindsay, Jack. *The Origins of Alchemy in Graeco-Roman Egypt*. London: F. Muller. 1970.

Lucas, A. *Ancient Egyptian Materials and Industries*. London: Edward Arnold. 1948.

Macrobius. *Commentary on the Dream of Scipio*. Trans. William Harris Stahl. New York: Columbia UP. 1952.

Macquer, Pierre. *Dictionnaire de Chymie*. Lacombe: Paris. 1766.

Magnus, Albertus. *Libellus de alchimia.* Trans. Sister Virginia Heines. Berkeley: University of California Press. 1958.

——. *The Compound of Compounds.* Trans. Luc Villeneuve. Glasgow: Hermetic Research Series No. 14. 2003.

Maier, Michael. *Atalanta Fugiens*. 1618. Basel: Barenreiter Verlag. 1964.

——. *Atalanta Fugiens: An Edition of the Emblems, Fugues and Epigrams.* Trans. and Ed. Joscelyn Godwin. Grand Rapids: Phanes Press. 1989.

Magdalino, Paul, and Maria V. Mavroudi. *The Occult Sciences in Byzantium*. Geneva: La Pomme D'or. 2006.

Mangetti, J.J. *Bibliotheca Chemica Curiosa*. Bologna: Arnaldo Forni. 1976.

Martelli, Matteo. *The Four Books of Pseudo-Democritus. Sources of Alchemy and Chemistry*. Ambix Vol. 60, Supp. 1. Leeds. 2013.

McLean, Adam. *The Silent Language: The Symbols of Hermetic Philosophy*. Amsterdam: Pelikaan. 1994.

Merkel, Ingrid, and Allen G. Debus. *Hermeticism and the Renaissance: Intellectual History and the Occult in Early Modern Europe*. Washington: Folger Shakespeare Library. 1988.

Moretti, Cesare. *Glossario del vetro veneziano*. Venezia: Marsilio Editori. 2001.

Moretti, Cesare and Trullio Toninato. *Ricette vetrarie del Rinascimento*. Venezia: Marsilio Editori. 2001.

Morienus. *The Book of the Composition of Alchemy*. Ed. Adam McLean. Glasgow: Hermetic Research Series No. 10. 2002.

Morienus. *A Testament of Alchemy; Being the Revelations of Morienus, Ancient Adept and Hermit of Jerusalem, to Khālid Ibn Yazīd Ibn Mu'āwiya, King of the Arabs, of the Divine Secrets of the Magisterium and Accomplishment of the Alchemical Art*. Trans. Lee Stavenhagen. Hanover, NH: Brandeis UP. 1974.

Multhauf, Robert Phillip. *The Origins of Chemistry*. N.p.: n.p. 1966.

Nasr, Seyyed Hossein. *An Introduction to Islamic Cosmological Doctrines*. Albany: SUNY Press. 1993.

Newman, William R. *The Summa Perfectionis of Pseudo-Geber: A Critical Edition, Translation and Study*. Leiden: E. J. Brill. 1991.

Nikodimos, St.: St. Makarios. *The Philokalia*. Trans. G.E.H. Palmer, Philip Sherrard, Kallistos Ware. London: Faber and Faber. 1983.

Nonnos. *Dionysiaca. Vol. 1*. Trans. W.H.D. Rouse. Cambridge: Harvard UP. 1984.

Norbu, Nomkhai. *Dream Yoga and the Practice of Natural Light*. Ithaca: Snow Lion. 1992.

Oppian. *Cynegetica*. Trans. A.W. Mair. Cambridge: Harvard UP. 1963.

Ovid. *Metamorphoses*. Trans. Frank Miller. Cambridge: Harvard UP. 1984.

Palacios, Felix. *Palestra-Pharmaceutica Chymica-Galenica*. Madrid: Ibara. 1768.

Palamas, St. Gregory. *Gregory Palamas. The Triads*. NJ: Paulist Press. 1983

Panofsky, Erwin. *Studies in Iconology*. New York: Harper & Row. 1972.

——. *Perspective as Symbolic Form*. New York: Zone Books. 1997.

Paracelsus. *The Hermetic and Alchemical Writings of Paracelsus*. A.E. Waite ed. New Hyde Park: University Books. 1967.

Partington, J.R., *Origins and Development of Applied Chemistry*. London: Longmans, Green. 1935.

Patai, Raphael. *The Jewish Alchemists: A History and Source Book*. Princeton: Princeton UP. 1994.

Pernety, Antoine Joseph. *Les Fables Egyptiennes et Grecques*. Paris: Archè. 1971.

——. *Dictionnaire Mytho-Hermétique*. Paris: Archè. 1980.

Petrus of Ferrara Bonus. *The New Pearl of Great Price.* New York: Arno Press. 1974.

Philalethes, Eirenaeus. *The Alchemical Works of Eirenaeus Philalethes*. S.M. Broddle ed. Boulder: Cinnabar Press. 1994.

Pico della Mirandola, Giovanni. *Heptaplus: Or, Discourse on the Seven Days of Creation*. New York: Philosophical Library. 1977.

Pinker, Steven. *The Language Instinct.* New York: Harper Perennial. 2007.

Plato. *Plato: Complete Works.* Ed. John Cooper. Indianapolis: Hackett. 1997.

Pliny. *Natural History* Vol. 5. Trans. H. Rackham. Cambridge: Harvard UP. 1971.

Plotinus. *The Enneads*. Trans. A.H. Armstrong. Cambridge: Harvard UP. 1984.

——. *The Enneads*. Trans. Stephen MacKenna. Burdett, NY: Larson Publications. 1992.

Plutarch. *Moralia Book VIII.* Trans. F.C. Babbitt. Cambridge: Harvard UP. 1949.

Popper, Karl. *The Logic of Scientific Discovery*. New York: Routledge. 2002.

Price, Michael. *Renaissance Mysteries. Vol I. Colour, Vol. II. Proportion and Composition*. New York: Michael Price Inc. 2017.

Proclus. *The Commentaries of Proclus on the Timaeus of Plato.* Trans. Thomas Taylor. London. 1820.

——. *A Commentary on the First Book of Euclid's Elements.* Trans. Glenn Morrow. Princeton: Princeton UP. 1992.

Pythagoras. *The Golden Verses of Pythagoras*. Trans. Antoine Fabre D'Olivet. New York: G.P. Putnam's Sons. 1917.

——. *Pythagorean Sourcebook and Library.* Trans. Kenneth S. Guthrie. Ed. David Fideler. Grand Rapids: Phanes Press. 1988.

Richards, John F. *Theophrastus on Stones*. Columbus: Ohio State U. 1956.

Ripley, Sir George. *The Compound of Alchymy*. London 1591. Norwood, NJ: Walter J. Johnson, Inc. Orbis Terranum. 1977.

Robinson, James M., ed. *Nag Hammadi Library*. San Francisco: Harper. 1990.

Roob, Alexander. *Alchemy and Mysticism*. Köln: Taschen. 2001.

Roscoe, Henry-Enfield. *A Treatise on Chemistry*. London: Macmillan. 1890.

Ruland, Martin. *A Lexicon of Alchemy*. Trans. A.E. Waite. Maine: Weiser. 1984.
Rupescissa, John of. *De Consideratione Quintae Essentie rerum omnium, opus...* Basile. 1561.
——. *Trattato sulla Quintessenza*. Trans. Stefano Andreani. Rome: Mediterranee. 1998.
Ruska, Julius. *Arabische Alchemisten*. Wiesbaden: M. Sändig. 1967.
Sacks, Oliver. *Hallucinations*. New York: Vintage Books. 2012.
Salaman, Clement, and Mahé. *The Way of Hermes: New Translations of The Corpus Hermeticum and the Definitions of Hermes Trismegistus to Asclepius*. Rochester: Inner Traditions. 2004.
Savonarola, Michele. *Libellus de aqua ardenti*. Pisa. 1484.
Schimmel, Annemarie. *Mystical Dimensions of Islam*. Chapel Hill: U of North Carolina. 1975.
Sendler, Egon. *The Icon Image of the Invisible*. Trans. S. Bigham. Oakwood Publications. 1995.
Siggel, Alfred. *Decknamen in Der Arabischen Alchemistischen Literatur*. Berlin: Akademie-Verlag. 1951.
Steele, R and D.W. Singer. "The Emerald Tablet." *Proceedings of the Royal Society of Medicine*. Vol. 21. 1928.
Smith, Cyril Stanley, and John G. Hawthorne. *Mappae Clavicula: A Little Key to the World of Medieval Techniques*. Philadelphia: American Philosophical Society. 1974.
Šprenger, Jaromír, and Josef Veselý. *Lékařsko-chymické a Alchymické Orákulum*. Praha: Půdorys. 1995.
Stapelton, H. E., R.F. Azo, Hidaya Husein. "Chemistry in Iraq and Persia in the 10th Century AD." *Memoirs of the Asiatic Society of Bengal*. Vol VIII, No 6, 1927.
Stapelton, H. E. "An Alchemical Compilation of the Thirteenth Century." *Memoirs of the Asiatic Society of Bengal*, 3, 1910.
Suhrawardi. *The Shape of Light*. Interpreted by Shaykh Tosun Bayrak al-Jerrahi. Louisville: Fons Vitae. 2006.
Synesios. *On Dreams by Saint Synesios*. Trans. Isaac Myer. Philadelphia: Myer. 1888.
Taylor, Thomas. *The Eleusinian and Bacchic Mysteries*. New York: De Vinne Press. 1891.
Theophrastus. *Theophrastus on Stones*. Trans. E. Caley and J. Richards. Columbus: Ohio State University. 1956.
Trismosin, Salomon. *Splendor Solis*. Facsimile reproduction. Köln: Krewel-Werke GMBH. 1972.
——. *Splendor Solis*. Trans. Joscelyn Godwin. Grand Rapids: Phanes Press. 1991.

——. *Splendor Solis*. Trans. Patrick Smith. Sequim: J.D. Holmes. 2000.

TsongKhapa. *TsongKhapa's Six Yogas of Naropa*. Trans. Glenn Mullin. Ithaca: Snow Lion. 1996.

Ulstad, Philip. *Coelum philosophorum*. Friburgi Helvetiroum. 1525.

Valentine, Basil. *The Triumphal Chariot of Antimony*. Trans. A.E. Waite. London: Vincent Stuart, Ltd. 1962.

——. *Azoth, ou Le Moyen du Faire l'Or caché des Philosophes*. 1659. Genova: Edition Anastatique. 1976.

van den Broek, Roelof; W. J. Hanegraaff. *Gnosis and Hermeticism from Antiquity to Modern Times*. New York: SUNY Press. 1998.

de Villanova, Arnald. *Liber de Vinis*. (ca 1310).

——. *Arnaldi de Villanova Opera Medica Omnia II Aphorismi de Gradibus*. Ed. Michael McVaugh. Universidad de Barcelona. Granada- Barcelona. 1975.

——. *Rosarium Philosophorum*. Trans. Patrick Smith. Edwards: Holmes Publishing. 2003.

Waite, Arthur Edward. *The Turba Philosophorum*. New York: Weiser. 1970.

——. *The Hermetic Museum*. New York: Weiser. 1974.

Wallace, B. Alan. *Choosing Reality*. Ithaca: Snow Lion Publications. 1996.

Wangyal, Tenzin. *The Tibetan Yogas of Dream and Sleep*. Ithaca: Snow Lion. 1998.

Wright, M.R. *Cosmology in Antiquity*. New York: Routledge. 1996.

Yates, Francis A. *The Art of Memory*. Chicago: University of Chicago Press. 1966.

——. *Giordano Bruno and the Hermetic Tradition*. Chicago: University of Chicago Press. 1991.

Zosimus. *Zosimos of Panopolis On the Letter Omega*. Trans. Howard Jackson. Missoula: Scholars Press. 1978.

——. *Zosime De Panopolis, Mémoires Authentiques*. Trans. Michèle Mertens. Paris: Les Belles Lettres. 1995.

——. *Muṣḥaf as-Ṣuwar. The Book of Pictures*. Theordor Abt ed. Einsiedeln: Daimon Publications. 2007.

ILLUSTRATIONS

All illustrations are my own except as noted below.

THEORIA

SILENCE
THE FIRST COMPANION

KOSMOS: AN EVER-LIVING FIRE

ONE IS ALL, ALL HAS ONE

NATURE DELIGHTS IN NATURE

NATURE CONQUERS NATURE

NATURE RULES NATURE

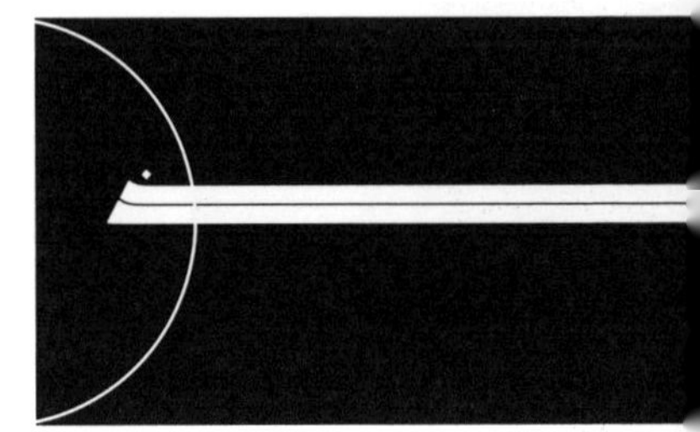

لوح الزمن

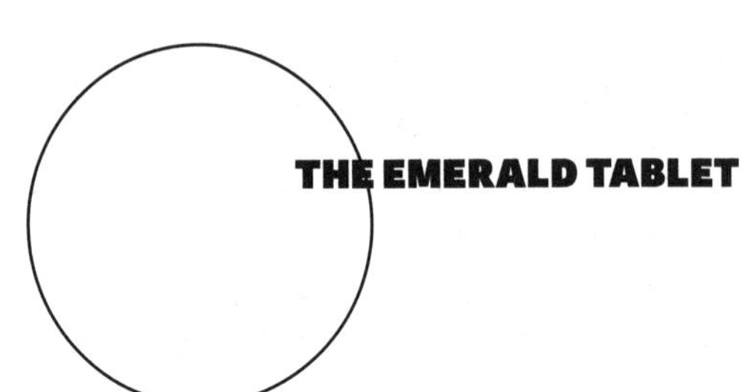

THE EMERALD TABLET

A Truth without doubt, wholly sound,
  that the highest is from the lowest
    and the lowest is from the highest.

The working of wonders is from the one,
  just as all things came from the one,
    by a single governance.

    Its father is the Sun and its mother is the Moon.
    The wind carries it in her belly.
    The Earth nourishes it.

Father of talismans,
  treasure-house of wonders,
    perfection of powers.

    Fire became earth.
    Separate the earth from the fire.
    The subtler is nobler than the gross.

With skilled work and restraint
  it will ascend from the Earth to Heaven
    and descend to Earth from Heaven.

And within itself is the power of the highest and of the lowest,
  within it is the light of lights,
    therefore darkness flees from it.

Power of powers.
  It can conquer every subtle thing,
    and penetrate everything gross.

Following the creation of the Macrocosm, the Work is completed.

This is my glory, and for that was Hermes named Thrice with Wisdom.

IF YOU WANT TO UNDERSTAND IT FROM EXPERIENCE, NOTICE WHAT HAPPENS WHEN YOU WISH TO BEGET.

Corpus Hermeticum XI.14

UNITY OF BEING.

ACTS OF CREATION.

THIS IS WHAT IT IS ABOUT.

The *Emerald Tablet* is a short alchemical text attributed to Hermes Trismegistus, the sage who brought arts, sciences, and the pursuit of wisdom to humanity. The *Emerald Tablet* is about the cyclic flow of creation – all creation, regardless of the scale or time of the composition. It attests to the truth of unity and the act of creation. This is its central point. All else flows from this vision.

And so it begins, with a declaration of truth.

A Truth without doubt, wholly sound,

The Arabic version translated here is found in the *Sirr al-Khalīqah*[1], *The Secret of Creation.* It is an apparent Arabic translation of an unknown Greek work by Apollonius translated around the early 9th century. The source text of the *Emerald Tablet* has not yet been found, so it isn't known for sure if the Arabic version is a translation. There are, however, indications in the piece that it was translated from a Greek work. There is no definitive proof of this, but the text itself is of a piece with the hermetic, gnostic and alchemical context of Greco-Roman Alexandria in the first several centuries of our era.
The *Sirr al-Khalīqah* is a work that explains the spheres of creation, laying out what was then known about the cosmos. It is fitting that the *Emerald Tablet*, a very brief composition about creation and the creative process, is found at the end. Summing up the relations within creation, The *Emerald Tablet*, describes the cyclic flow of creation:

that the highest is from the lowest
and the lowest is from the highest.

1 Ursula Weisser ed. *Kitāb Sirr al-Khalīqah wa Ṣan'at al-Ṭabī'a.* (Aleppo. 1979) 524.

If all things are parts of god, then all things are god, and he makes himself in making things. His making can never cease because he is ceaseless. And as god has no end, so his making has neither beginning nor end. *Corpus Hermeticum. XVI.18.*

Often phrased, "as above so below, as below so above,"[2] it has become the most recognizable phrase from the *Emerald Tablet*. Look again at the Arabic from the *Sirr al- Khalīqah*. "The above is from the below and the below is from the above." The Arabic *min* means from, of, belonging to, and consisting of, as in made of a material or coming from somewhere. We can say in Arabic, Latin and English, that something is from somewhere, or that it is made from something. Either way, this line in the Apollonius versions expresses a rather radical notion, more than just a similitude, more than they are like each other as in the vulgate version the one that reads, "as above so below...". Rather, that the heavens are made of the below, the sublunary, and that the sublunary is made from the heavens – that they originate one from the other. This suggests a view of the cosmos in constant generation, constant unfolding, and constant devouring – an eternal becoming at every moment, an endless creation whose source and destination is, as it were, the one.

(The world) was ever, is now, and ever shall be an ever-living fire. *Heraclitus. Fragment 20*

The highest is from the lowest and the lowest is from the highest.

All things exist eternally through the cycle of generation, and the equilibrium among them all is maintained by its balancing destruction. *Proclus. A Commentary on the First Book of Euclid's Elements 119.*

Although the earliest extant Arabic manuscript states it this way, and my own take on it is that it is the correct version, we cannot dismiss the later Latin versions as incorrect, as they may be simply different versions of an Arabic, Syriac, or Greek text. And in opening up this statement to get a more complete picture as to its possible meanings, I will consider this same line from several other Latin texts.

One such version, a 13th century *Emerald Tablet*, is found in *Secretus Secretorum*[3] of pseudo-Aristotle. It states:

2 The Latin translation of the *Sirr al-Khalīqah* by Hugh of Santalla, translates it as "from" as well. "Superiora de inferioribus, inferiora de superioribus." "The above is from the below, the below is from the above." Françoise Hudry ed. "De secretis nature du ps.-Apollonius de Tyane." Chrysopoeia Tome VI (1997-1999) 152. For this and other early texts see pages 55ff.

3 In: S.Gentile, and Carlos Gilly. *Marsilio Ficino E Il Ritorno Di Ermete Trismegisto.* (Florence: Centro Di, 1999) 199. From Secretus *Secretorum Pseudo-Aristotle. 13th Century* ms. Plut. 83 Sup. 2, 23v. Biblioteca Laurenziana.

Quod inferiora superioribus et superiora inferioribus respondent.

That the inferior responds to the superior and the superior to the inferior.

There are reflections of the incorporeals in corporeals and of corporeals in incorporeals. *Corpus Hermeticum. XVII.1.*

Here generation is expressed as a cause and effect, a call and response, a resonance. This implies a reciprocal effect: an object that is acted on by a force has a reciprocal effect on the subject, or agent, of the action being undertaken; or a *corresponding* aspect, that is, there is something below and it corresponds or answers to something above with the shade of meaning of similitude.

Nature is the mirror of truth; the latter is at once the body of the incorporeal and the light of the invisible. The generous nature of this world teaches all. If it seems to you that nothing is a vain work, you will find the work and the craftsman. *From Hermes Trismegistus to Asclepius: Definitions.8.5. The Way of Hermes. p114-15.*

Another example, the vulgate edition, which comes from *Liber hermetis alchimie*[4] was, and still is, the most widely known of all the Latin translations, reads slightly differently.

Quod est superius est sicut quod inferius, et quod inferius* est sicut quod *est superius.

That which is above is like that which is below, and that which is below is like that which is above.

Est sicut quod translates into *as that/like that/just as/so as/that which.* The link of similarity leads us to ask the question, "like in what way?"

The Golden Verses[5] of Pythagoras, observes that, "Nature, alike in everything, is the same in everyplace." That similarity is explained by an underlying unity. The same idea is also expressed in one of the basic assumptions of modern physics and cosmology that the physical laws that apply here and now also apply elsewhere regardless of space, distance, or time. Take for example the speed of light. That theory, as of the early 21st century, proposes that under the same conditions, the speed of light is the same here as on the other side of Earth or 100 miles above, or across the galaxy, or across the universe. It is the same today

4 Arundel ms. Steele and Singer. "The Emerald Tablet." *Proceedings of the Royal Society of Medicine.* Vol. 21. (1928) 492.

5 Antoine Fabre D'Olivet, Pythagoras. *The Golden Verses of Pythagoras.* (New York: G.P. Putnam's Sons, 1917) 128. line 28.

or 200 years ago or moments after the creation – the Big Bang singularity. This is an assumption that physics makes and needs to make. There is no way to actually test this – it is an assumption, a statement, an axiom. In other words, it is a metaphysical statement, a very useful assumption, but still metaphysical.

There is another sense of likeness that is the generative aspect. Consider how siblings, sharing origins, are similar to each other and to their parents. One set of causes produces multiple results but similar to each other, aspects of the same larger phenomenon or cause. We see an example of this in the myth of Aphrodite's birth – the castration of Uranus, his genitals tossed into the sea gave birth from the ensuing foam to Aphrodite (sea-foam) and "her animal of love,"[6] the nautilus. Here "likeness" between two created things arises from the same union creating, in essence, twins.

Here conspires with There and There with Here, elaborating together the consistency and eternity of a Cosmos and by their correspondences revealing the sequence of things to the trained observer. *Plotinus. Enneads. III.3.6.*

Another way to understand similitude is to flip the arrow of causation. Instead of one union creating likenesses, "likeness," itself, according to Proclus, "is sufficient to join beings to one another."[7] It is this last sense of *likeness* that the vulgate version of the *Emerald Tablet* emphasizes – the sense of similitude rather than of generation. It links the upper and lower by likeness. There are parallels to the events in the Heavens and the events on Earth and these parallels are what link them.

But the deeper link is the idea of continuous creation exemplified in the Arabic "the highest is from the lowest and the lowest is from the highest."

The *Emerald Tablet* continues:

The working of wonders is from the one,
just as all things came from the one,[8]
by a single governance.

6 "And he himself sprung from the blood of Uranus together with Aphrodite, the pompilus (the argonaut) is an animal of love." Aristonicus commentary on the Illiad, quoted in: Pavel Florenskiĭ, Nicoletta Misler, and Wendy R. Salmond. *Beyond Vision: Essays on the Perception of Art.* (London: Reaktion, 2002) 172.

7 "On the Hieratic Art." Translation by Brian Copenhaver in Merkel, Ingrid and Allan Debus. *Hermeticism and the Renaissance.* (Washington:Folger, 1988) 79–110.

8 In another edition of the work *jawhar al waḥīd* – one essential nature, substance as opposed to form in the Aristotelian sense.

Creation flows from the one, and like language, like speech, there is first an undifferentiated stream, then an articulation, then a naming and finally a composition. Here we can understand creation as the saying of the one.

It is wise to listen not to me but to the word, and confess that all things are one. *Heraclitus, On The Universe. 471*

This idea that from the one all things arise is a hermetic idea found throughout the *Corpus Hermeticum* and Greek philosophy.

"One is all, and through it is all, and to it all, and if it has not all, all is nothing,"[9] reads the outer ring of an emblem found in Κλεοπατρις χρυςοποιια, *Kleopatra's Gold Making,*[10] an alchemical text composed around the 1st century CE. In it, the idea of unity and origin out of unity are stated verbally and iconically. The inner ring reads, "One is the serpent having its venom according to two compositions," an allusion to the creative duality, as well as a stage of a physical process.

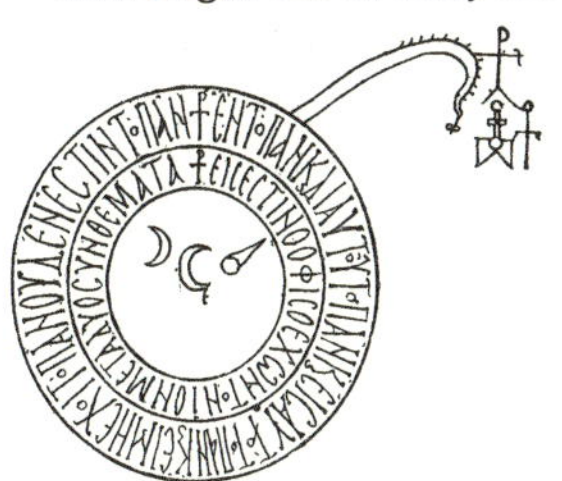

Now the Monad, which is the origin and root of all things, is present in all things, as root and origin. *Corpus Hermeticum Vol. I p53 (Nock and Festugiere paragraph 10).*

On the same page we see the ouroboros, the serpent biting its tail, encircling the phrase "One is all." The ouroboros represents the boundary, the first duality out of one. In this single image we see the idea of endless self-creation.

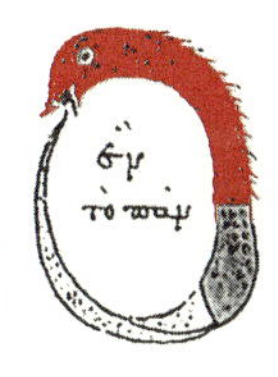

This "one" is the un-created unity from which all creation, both the creation of the cosmos and the creation of works of wonder, comes. What are these wonders, these marvels that the *Emerald Tablet* speaks of creating? The answer is in the use of the plural. It is not just one work but many works, "...just as all things come from the one by one governance."[11]

Kmeph, an intellect thinking himself, and turning his thoughts towards himself [...] it must be specified, is worshipped by means of silence alone. *Iamblichus. On The Mysteries. VIII.3.263.*

9 Εν το παν και δι αυτου το παν και εις αυτο το παν και ει μη εχοι το παν ουδεν εστιν το παν. "The all is one; and the all is through it and the all is into it, and if the all did not have the all, it would be nothing." Or "The all is one, through which all exists and through it and in it is the all" In the center are the signs for the Moon/Silver, Mercury/mercury, and the Sun/Gold. At the end of the Snake tail is a cluster of mysterious glyphs the meanings of which are uncertain.

10 M. Berthelot. *Collection des ancien alchimistes grecs* Vol. I. (Paris: Steinheil, 1887) 132–34.

11 تدبير Tadbīr– Regulation, design, handling with care, proceed in a well-planned and prudent manner. The Latin struggles with the rather bureaucratic *consilii administratione*, the adminstration of counsel. Process is too matter-of-fact, sounding like an algorithm to be followed. Governance I think best captures the sense.

This means that the Work, the Opus Magnum, or for that matter any creative act, follows the same governance, the same process as the creation of the universe. But what is the process? An answer can be found in *The Book of Komarios*, also written around the first century. In it, Ostanes, a quasi-mythic figure in early alchemy, asks Kleopatra our question:

Death has to do with destruction, yet none of the things in the cosmos is destroyed. *Corpus Hermeticum. VIII.1.*

> ***...Tell us how the highest descends to the lowest and how the lowest ascends to the highest and how the intermediate approaches the highest and the lowest and how the parts do not separate in advancing and being united to the intermediate and which of the elements belongs to them; also how the blessed waters descend to visit the dead who lie prostrate; shackled and afflicted in darkness and gloom within Hades and how the medicine of life penetrates and awakens them...***[12]

And from the same work:

> ***...And while seeking the beautiful philosophy we found it divided into four parts and discovered the generic nature of each thing. In the first part it covers the process of making black, in the second that of making white, in the third that of making yellow and in the fourth that of making violet. ...here between the processes of making black, white, yellow and violet there is the maceration and the washing of the species of things.***[13]

Practically speaking, this is a circulation process during which the prima materia, the matter being worked on, is brought through color changes that signify a change of the material itself, a transmutation of ordinary matter into a philosophical state or station. The process I outline here is explored in more detail in a later chapter. The instrument is a basic circulation apparatus often referred to as a *kerotakis* (from the Greek artist's instrument used in encaustic painting).

12 Berthelot. Vol 3, 292. Unpublished translation C.A. Browne. *C.A. Browne Papers* Mss Col 418 NYCPL.
13 Berthelot. Vol 3, 291.

The divine water[14] is placed in the lower flask referred to as Hades; in the upper chamber a leaf of metal alloy, the prima materia, is placed upon a grid (the kerotakis). The lower flask is heated and the vapor rises, cools, and condenses in the upper chamber acting on the leaf. It then flows back down to Hades, is heated once again and so circulates in this manner. As the work proceeds, with intermediary steps between circulations, the prima materia is reduced to black, then changes from black to white, to yellow, and finally, to violet. This final result is often called the powder of projection, and is able to effect transmutations.

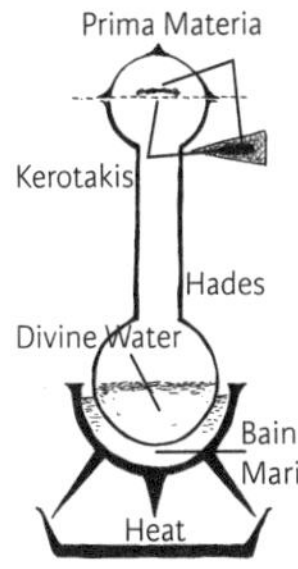

The way up and the way down is one and the same. *Heraclitus. Fragment 60*

For the numbers five and six alone exhibit the cyclic power by turning back upon them selves in the terms that are derived from them, since when they are multiplied, they end with themselves. *Proclus A Commentary on the First Book of Euclid's Elements. p120.*

The Book of Komarios continues:

> ***...how the blessed waters descend to visit the dead who lie prostrate; shackled and afflicted in darkness and gloom within Hades and how the medicine of life penetrates and awakens them so that they are aroused from sleep in their beds; also how the new waters penetrate, which are brought forth at the commencement of, and during, the confinement and which come with the light, a cloud bearing them aloft. And the cloud rises from the sea, bearing aloft the waters which, as they are made manifest, the philosophers delight to behold.***[15]

With this process in mind re-read the *Emerald Tablet*. Then consider this from *The Apocryphon of John*, a gnostic text, which recounts a three-fold cycle of descent into Hades and ascent to the Light. It ends with... "Still for a third time I went..."

Sage: When the many winds of the inside swirl up, they cause the cloud to ascend and the vapor of the sea arises. *Zosimos. Muṣḥaf as-Ṣuwar. The Book of Pictures. p513*

> ***...that I might enter into the midst of darkness and the inside of Hades. And I filled my face with the light of the completion of their aeon. And I entered into the midst of their prison, which is the prison of***

14 υδατοσ θεον (hudatos theon): sulphur water or divine water. It refers to a number of solutions, most commonly, a calcium polysulphide. For the full process see page 85.

15 Berthelot. Vol 3, 291.

the body. And I said, 'He who hears, let him get up from the deep sleep.' And he wept and shed tears. Bitter tears he wiped from himself and he said, 'Who is it that calls my name, and from where has this hope come to me, while I am in the chains of the prison?'[16]

The moon, nature's instrument, transforming the matter below, and in the midst of the universe is the earth, the nurse who feeds terrestrial creatures. *Corpus Hermeticum. XI.7.*

The specific use of language, the concepts of ascent and descent, the entrapment of spirit by matter and the stages toward perfection/awakening are used in the three texts – the *Emerald Tablet, The Book of Komarios* and *The Apocryphon of John.* We see within these texts the contours of language struggling to describe several aspects of creation with a hidden unity at their core. And it is not only in these works discussed here; we also find these ideas throughout the gnostic, hermetic, neoplatonic, and alchemical writings of Alexandria.

The next verse of the *Tablet* underscores the importance or fundamental nature of polarity. The previous verses allude to the metaphor of verticality, the following brings in the horizontal metaphor of Sun and Moon, Father and Mother.

Earth is the support of the world, the basis of the elements, the nurse of the living, the receptacle of the dead. *From Hermes Trismegistus to Asclepius: Definitions.1.3. The Way of Hermes. p110.*

Its Father is the Sun and its Mother is the Moon.
The wind carries it in her belly.
The Earth nourishes it.

The process shifts to the material world and another polarity arises. The image of Father/Mother and Sun/Moon suggests that duality is at the heart of creation. As the Corpus Hermeticum states: "...if you want to understand this in practice, watch what happens when you desire to beget."[17] Creation arises out of polarity, name the pairs what you will. A union is suggested, the loss of the two in becoming one in a third. This is the *creation of wonders*, this is the "*it*" referred to above. That "*it*" that is nourished by the Earth, that "it" carried by the Wind, that "it" whose Mother is the Moon, "it" whose Father

The world is time's receptacle; the cycling and stirring of time invigorate it. *Asclepius, 30. Hermetica.*

16 James M. Robinson, ed. *Nag Hammadi Library*. (San Francisco: Harper, 1990) 122.

17 *Corpus Hermeticum* XI.14. Salaman, Clement, and Mahé. *The Way of Hermes*. (Rochester, VT: Inner Traditions, 2004) 56.

is the Sun. "*It*" is *the creation of wonders.* And the unity of this process is the:

Father of talismans,
treasure-house of wonders,
perfection of powers.

It is the source of all creative action and results. The word translated here as *talisman* is a literal translation of the Arabic talismāt.[18] *Talismāt* itself is an Arabic rendering of the Greek τελεσμα (telesma), which in ancient Greek means completion or religious rite, and in Byzantine Greek the word has both those meanings, as well as "talisman" as it is currently used. This word in context should be read as a "result" or "completion" in the sense of a ritual – a physical manifestation, an object, or an assembly of objects (or even actions i.e. rituals) taking the imprint of the creative act – a talisman. This unity is again the source of things: manifest, but a symbol; the end point of creation; the ultimate possible. Manifestation, as it were, ends there and in its end is the seed of its return.

Fire became earth.
Separate the earth from the fire.
The subtler is nobler than the gross.

Light becomes material. The immaterial becomes concrete. Having followed the creative flow to its manifestation on/in Earth, we now come to the beginning of what could be understood as practical instructions: "Separate the Earth from the Fire." It suggests a reversing of the process to the "un-making" and releasing of the "spirit." In other words, open up the earth, the body, and let the fire free, or abstract the matter/earth from the fire. The return is to draw out light from matter. A sense

The human rises up to heaven and takes its measure and knows what is in its heights and its depths, and he understands all else exactly and – greater than all of this – he comes to be on high without leaving earth behind. *Corpus Hermeticum. X.25.*

18 I've left it as talisman, allowing the strangeness of the word to come through. It is also related to the word *teleste*, a purification rite or practice such as mathematics or the animation of statues. See also Proclus *"On the Hieratic Art."* Translation by Brian Copenhaver in Ingrid Merkel and Allen G. Debus. *Hermeticism and the Renaissance* (Washington: Folger. 1988) 79–110. See Cotnoir *On The Animation of Statues* (New York: Khepri Press).

The imagination, this intermediary essence, in yielding to the direction of the soul, [...] purifies itself and rises with it towards heaven. *On Dreams by Saint Synesios. p16, 17.*

of what this entails is found when we consider pigments used in writing holy icons. Minerals are ground, cleaned, worked, and massed together in a medium so that only color and light remain. As this light and color are worked and an image is formed, relationships arise amongst the forms and a narrative begins. Here, we see the ascent of meaning from matter. With this drawing out of light from matter, we realize a transfiguration, which allows for the possibility of transmutation to take place.

With skilled work and restraint
it will ascend from the Earth to Heaven
and descend to Earth from Heaven.

As the channels are mingled together (the highest life) perfects the works of imperishable fire. *Chaldean Oracles. Fragment 66*

And with this circulation the integration of the forces inherent in all is attained. What is the "*it*" that "ascends from the Earth to Heaven"? There is a suggestion of an answer in the *Corpus Hermeticum*. In Book 16:5, Asclepius, student of Hermes, says to King Ammon: "the craftsman (I mean the sun) binds heaven to earth, sending essence below and raising matter above."[19] Hermetically speaking, "*it*" is the "substance" of the Creator, as Asclepius stated. It is the spirit, the spark embedded in matter, confused in embodiment. It is the fifth element of space that permeates all creation – the quintessence. This is what circulates between heaven and earth, both literally in observing nature and metaphorically as a material practice. And so this verse can be understood as a description of the kerotakis process – the circulation of the Divine Water, its vapors interacting with the metal leaf. The subtle waters, the divine water, the intermediary between the high and the low mentioned in Kleopatra. And between these two meanings there is no real contradiction, perhaps in form only. Read across the texts and look for the echoes of the collisions between the material alchemical processes and the hermetic spiritual ideas.

19 One of the words that suggest a Greek original is talismāt. The Arabic *talismāt* (pl) *tilsam* (sg), is from the Byzantine Greek *telesma*. Another suggestion of a Greek original is the gender of the Sun and Moon. In Arabic, the Sun is feminine and the Moon is masculine, while in Greek the Sun is masculine and the Moon is feminine.

And within itself is the force of the highest and of the lowest.
within it is the light of lights,
therefore darkness flees from it.

Through the circulation, the virtues of the high and low are "absorbed." Darkness flees from it. The dirt, the extraneous, the impure, the darkness inherent in matter is dispelled, transmuting base things as light transmutes darkness. This is indeed the "power of powers." The final result contains the force of all it had encountered and the light of lights resides within it. One may say it resides in all things, but here, in its most perfected body, its powers are amplified and transmutational.

Power of powers.
it can conquer every subtle thing
and penetrate everything gross.

Like darkness changed to light, it has itself been changed and is now transmutational, overcoming every subtle thing – Air and Fire; and penetrates the densest matter – Water and Earth. The work has come to an end – the end result is not only an end, but can itself make changes in the world around it. It is the wave on which we ride, directing some of the flow. Or, more accurately, it is surfing amongst the flow, manipulating, inter-acting with the world around us. In its resistance to our actions, dialogue with the world begins. With each cut, we open up the matter, the body, the world, and articulate time and space. Through the interaction of subject and object we discover the web of relations, and, in changing the object through work or manipulation, the subject is also changed. Its identity is only an identity in relation to its object, and as the object changes, so does the subject. The object, thus worked or "alchemized," carries a memory of sorts: one that creates the final object through its chain of existence, the vaporous twistings of the relationships that give rise to the subject and the object. In this cycle it gains the power of powers, imprinting on the final object the experience of discovery or exploration in order to realize one's self in one's creation.

And the soul rejoices in her home, because after the body had been hidden in darkness, she found it filled with light, and she united with it, since it had become divine towards her, and it is now her home. For it had put on the right of divinity and darkness has departed from it. *Book of Komarios. IV xx. Section 15.*

Concrete creative acts, i.e., working with materials, make more explicit this idea of reciprocal effect: the striking, cutting, grinding of stone, metal or air, etc. With the articulation of the material through our hands, we develop articulations, or pathways, in our minds. And, as the penultimate line states, it is true of all creation regardless of the medium.

Following the creation of the macrocosm, the work is completed.

This is my glory, and for that was Hermes named Thrice with Wisdom.

If all things are parts of god, then all things are god, and he makes himself in making things. His making can never cease because he is ceaseless. And as god has no end, so his making has neither beginning nor end. *Corpus Hermeticum. XVI.18.*

The line ending with "*The Work is completed*" is to be read with the sense of, "The process, the creation of the *Work* follows, or is like, the process of the creation of the Great World, the Macrocosm, the Universe." This repeats the same idea given in the earlier line, *"The creation of wonders is from the one, just as all things come from the one by one process,"* and reinforces it. In fact, a variant manuscript of the *Sirr al-Khalīqah* reads, "Following the creation of the Macrocosm, the Microcosm and the Work are created."[20] It makes explicit the idea that creating, regardless of the medium so to speak, is the same on any scale. And not just what we might consider alchemy, but all sorts of wonders in all different fields and mediums.

Plotinus observes, "The arts do not simply imitate what they see, but they run back up to the forming principles from which nature derives."[21]

Having followed the creative flow to its manifestation, we now come to the return – to run back up to the forming principles and beyond. That is, reversing the process, un-making or unsaying, as it were, and releasing the fire/spirit. Since all creation is one, we can use any creative act to demonstrate these principles while engaging in an action meditation, where the

20 Weisser. 525. Footnote 5, Manuscript K.

21 Plotinus. *Ennead V*. Trans. A.H. Armstrong. (Cambridge. Harvard UP, 1984) 239.

act is both a meditation and a manifestation of the inner process. The actor, action, and object are defined by each other, arise from each other, and so are mirrored in each other and respond to each other. And through this work a certain grace of action comes with mastery over self and art.

Open up the earth, open the body, abstract and draw out light from matter – cycling from low to high, from high to low. And through this cycling of Earth to Heaven, and Heaven to Earth the integration of the forces inherent in both is attained. The final result contains the force of all it encountered and the revelation of the light of lights residing within. This is transfiguration. Heaven within, cycles of withdrawal and extension, deep meditation and action in the world, with the body becoming the locus of the ultimate result – the light of lights. In its most perfected body, its powers are amplified and transmutational. With this, the work has come to an apparent end – apparent because the end result is not only an end, but can itself effect change in the world around it. The extraneous, the dirt, the impure, the darkness inherent in matter is dispelled, transmuting base things as light transmutes darkness.

This is indeed the power of powers. Once one understands, all things are possible. Ask any artist.

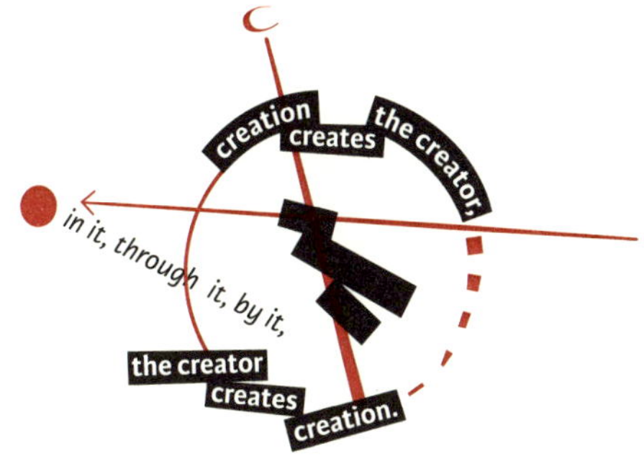

ألواح الزمرد

EMERALD TABLETS

لوح الزمرد

حَقٌّ لا شَكَّ فيهِ صَحيحٌ

إنَّ الأَعْلى مِنَ الأَسْفَلِ وَالأَسْفَلُ مِنَ الأَعْلى

عَمَلُ العَجائِبِ مِنْ واحِدٍ كَما كانَتْ الأَشياءُ كُلُّها مِنْ واحِدٍ بِتَدْبيرِ واحِدٍ،

أَبوهُ الشَّمْسُ، أُمُّهُ القَمَرُ،
حَمَلَتْهُ الرِّيحُ في بَطْنِها،
غَذَّتْهُ الأَرْضُ،

أَبو الطَّلِسْمات، خازِنُ العَجائِبِ، كامِلُ القوى،

نارٌ صارَتْ أَرْضاً أَعْزِلِ الأَرْضَ مِنَ النّارِ،

اللَطيفُ أَكْرَمُ مِنَ الغَليظِ،

بِرِفْقٍ وَحِكْمٍ يَصعَدُ مِنَ الأَرْضِ إلى السَّماءِ وَيَنْزِلُ إلى الأَرْضِ مِنَ السَّماءِ،

وَفيهِ قُوَّةُ الأَعْلى والأَسْفَلِ،

لِأَنَّ مَعَهُ نورَ الأَنْوارِ فَلِذلِكَ تَهْرُبُ مِنْهُ الظُّلْمَةُ،

قُوَّةُ القوى

يَغْلِبُ كُلَّ شَيءٍ لَطيفٍ، يَدْخُلُ في كُلِّ شَيءٍ غَليظٍ،

عَلى تَكْوينِ العالَمِ الأَكْبَرِ تَكَوَّنَ العَمَلُ،

فَهذا فَخْري وَلِذلِكَ سُمِّيتُ هِرمِس المُثَلَّثُ بِالحِكْمَةِ.

EMERALD TABLET

A Truth without doubt, wholly sound, that the highest is from the lowest and the lowest is from the highest. The working of wonders is from the one, just as all things came from the one, by a single governance. **Its father is the Sun and its mother is the Moon. The wind carries it in her belly. The Earth nourishes it.** Father of talismans, treasure-house of wonders, perfection of powers. Fire became earth. Separate the earth from the fire. The subtler is nobler than the gross. With skilled work and restraint it will ascend from the Earth to Heaven and descend to Earth from Heaven. And within itself is the power of the highest and of the lowest, **within it is the light of lights, therefore darkness flees from it. Power of powers. It can conquer every subtle thing,** and penetrate everything gross. Following the creation of the Macrocosm, the Work is completed. This is my glory, and for that was Hermes named Thrice with Wisdom.

Kitāb Sirr al-Khalīqah wa Ṣan'at al-Ṭabī'a. Apollonius of Tyanna

TABULA SMARAGDINA

hac verborum intricata veritate descriptam... **Superiora de inferioribus, inferiora de superioribus. Prodigiorum operatio ex uno, quemadmodum omnia ex uno eodemque ducunt originem una eademque consilii administratione.** ***Cujus pater Sol, mater vero Luna.*** **Eam ventus in corpore suo extollit, terra fit dulcior. Vos ergo praestigiorum filii, prodigiorum opifices, discretione perfecti, Si terra fiat, eam ex igne subtili, qui omnem grossitudinem et quod hebes est antecellit, spaciosus et prudentia et sapientiae industria educite. A terra ad caelum conscendet, a caelo ad terram dilabitur, superiorum et inferiorum vim continens atque potentiam. Unde omnis ex eodem illuminatur obscuritas. Cujus videlicet potentia quicquid subtilis est transcendit et rem grossam totum ingreditur.**

Quae quidem operatio secundum majoris mundi

compositionem habet subsistere.

Quod videlicet Hermes philosophus triplicem sapientiam vel triplicem scientiam appellat.

De secretis nature. Apollonius of Tyana

with this truth, entangled in words, inscribed... The higher is from the lower. The lower is from the higher. The working of wonders **comes from the one,** as all things originate together from one and the same, by the same governance. *Whose father is the Sun, but whose mother, the Moon.* The wind lifts it up in its own body, the Earth becomes sweeter. You therefore, sons of deceptions, workers of wonders, of perfect discretion, if it should become earth, lead it out of fire which surpasses all grossness and what is ponderous, draw it forth expansively & prudently & by the hard work of wisdom. **From the Earth,** it will rise to the Heaven, it will slip down from Heaven to Earth,containing the force and potential of the higher and lower things. Therefore from out of the same thing all obscurity is illuminated. Namely, whose power transcends whatever is subtle and enters whole into gross matter.

This operation indeed, has its being according to

the composition of the greater world.

Hermes Philosopher calls this namely, three-fold

wisdom, or, three-fold knowledge.

لَوْحُ الزُّمُــرُّذِ

حقّـًا يقينًا لا شَكَّ فيهِ إذْ كانَ الأَعْلى مِنَ
الأَسْفَلِ وَالأَسْفَلُ مِنَ الأَعْلى عَمَلُ العَجايِبِ
مِنْ واحِدٍ كما كانَتْ الأَشيَاءُ كُلُّها مِنْ واحِدٍ
وَأَبوهُ الشَّمْسُ وَأُمُّهُ القَـمَرُ حَمَلَتْهُ الأَرضُ في
بَطْنِهَا وَغَذَّتْهُ الرِّيحُ في بَطْنِها نارًا صارَتْ أرْضًا
أَغذوا الأَرضَ مِنَ اللَطيف بِقُوَّةِ القُوى يَصْعَدُ
مِنَ الأَرْضِ إلى السماءِ فَيَكونُ مُسَلَّطًا عَلى

الأَعْلى والأَسْفَلِ

E T

Truly, there is no doubt in it. Thus it was, *the highest is from the lowest* **and the lowest from the highest.** The working of wonders is from the one, just as all things come from the one. Its father is the Sun. Its mother is the Moon. **The Earth carries it in her belly.** And the wind nourishes it in her belly, as Fire becoming Earth. Nourish the Earth with the subtle, through the power of powers, and *it will ascend from the Earth to the Heaven* and become one given authority over

the highest and the lowest.

Kitāb Usṭuqus al-Uss. Book of the Foundation of the Elements.
Jābir ibn Hayyān

Et pater vester Hermogenes qui triplex est philosophia optime philosophando dixit: veritas ita se habet et non est dubium, quod inferiora superioribus et superiora inferioribus respondent. Operator miraculorum est unus solus deus, a quo descendit omnis operatio mirabilis. **SIC OMNES RES CREANTUR AB UNA SOLA SUBSTANTIA, ET UNA SOLA DISPOSITIONE.** Cuius pater est sol, cuius mater est luna. Que portavit ipsam naturam per auram in utero, terra privata impregnata est ab ea. Hinc dicitur sol pater incantamentorum causatorum et thesaurus miraculorum et largitor virtutum. Ex igne facta est terra. Separa terrenum ab igneo, quia subtiliter dignius est grosso et rarum spisso. Hoc fit sapienter et discrete. Ascendit enim de terra in caelum, et ruit de celo in terram. et non interficit superiores et inferiores virtutem. Sic ergo dominatur inferioribus et superioribus et tu dominaberis sursum et deorsum. **TECUM ENIM EST LUX LUMINUM, ET PROPTER HOC FUGIUNT A TE OMNES TENEBRE. VIRTUS SUPERIOR VINCIT OMNIA.** Omne enim rarum agit in densum. Secundum dispositionem maioris mundi, currit hec operatio. Et propter hoc vocatur Hermogenes triplex in phylosphia.

Secretus Secretorum. Pseudo-Aristotle

And your father Hermogenes who is thrice greatest in philosophy, philosophizing in the best possible way, said: The truth is this way and there is no doubt that the lower things answer to the higher things and the higher to the lower. The maker of miracles is just one god, from whom descends every miraculous activity. **THUS ALL THINGS ARE CREATED FROM ONLY ONE SUBSTANCE AND ONLY ONE ARRANGEMENT.** Whose father is the sun, whose mother is the moon. The wind carries the nature itself in its uterus, the private earth has been impregnated by it. Because of this it is called the father of spells, effects, the treasury of miracles and the bestower of virtues. From fire earth is made. Separate the earthen from the fiery, because it is more dignified, in a subtle way, than the gross. (and the rare is more dignified than the gross.) This is done with wisdom and discernment, for it ascends from earth to heaven and it falls from the heavens to the earth. And it does not destroy the higher and lower by its power. And so it rules over the lower and the higher and you will rule over the upward and the downward. **FOR THE LIGHT OF LIGHTS IS WITH YOU INDEED AND BECAUSE OF THIS, ALL DARKNESS FLEES FROM YOU. THE HIGHER CONQUERS ALL.** For every fine thing acts upon the dense. According to the arrangement of the greater world so this work runs. Because of this, Hermogenes is called triple in philosophy.

Verum, sine mendacio, certum et certissimum: Quod est superius est sicut quod inferius, et quod inferius est sicut quod est superius, ad preparanda miracula rei unius. Sicut res omnes ab una fuerunt, meditatione unius, et sic sunt natae res omnes ab hac una re aptatione. *Pater ejus sol. Mater ejus luna. Portavit illuc ventus in ventre suo. Nutrix ejus terra est.* Pater omnis telesmi tocius mundi hic est. Vis ejus integra est. Si versa fuerit in terram separabit terram ab igne, subtile ab spisso. Suaviter cum magno ingenio ascendit a terra in cœlom. Iterum descendit in terram, et recipit vim superiorem atque inferiorem. Sic habebis gloriam claritatis mundi. Ideo fugiet a te omnis obscuritas. Hic est tocius fortitudinis fortitudo fortis, quia vincet omnem rem subtilem, omnemque rem solidam penetrabit.

Sicut hic mundus creatus est.

Hinc erunt aptationes mirabiles quarum mos hic est. Itaque vocatus sum Hermes, tres tocius mundi partes habens sapientie.

Et completum est quod diximus de opere solis.

Liber Hermetis de alchimia.

True, without lie, certain and most certain. That which is above is like to that which is below, and that which is below is like that which is above, to accomplish the miracles of one thing. And as all things were from the one by meditation of the one, thus all things are born from this one thing by one adaptation. *The father thereof is the sun, its mother the moon. The wind carried it in its womb. Its nurse is the earth.* The father of all works of wonder in the whole world is here. Its power is complete. If it be cast to earth, it will separate the earth from fire, the subtle from the gross. Gently and with great ingenuity it ascends from earth to heaven. And it again descends into the earth and receives the powers of the higher and lower things. Thus you will have the glory of the whole world. All obscurity will fly from you. This is the strong fortitude of all strength, for it overcomes every subtle thing and will penetrate every solid thing.

Thus the world was created.

From this will be marvelous adaptations, of which this is the method. Therefore I am called Hermes, having the three parts of the wisdom of the whole world.

What I have said of the Solar Work is complete.

FILIUS: PATER, QUID EST DIGNIUS ALTERO, AN ESSE COELUM VEL TERRAM?

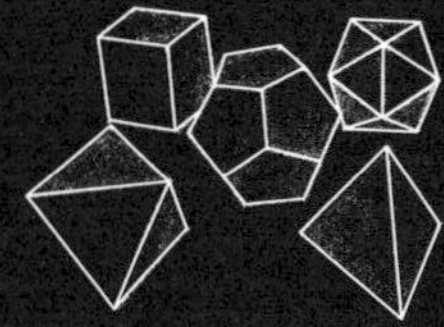

RESPONDIT, UTERQUE ALTERO INDIGET: MEDIOCRE ENIM PROPOSITUM EST PRAECETIS.

FILIUS: PATER, QUID EST DIGNIUS ALTERO, AN ESSE COELUM VEL TERRAM?

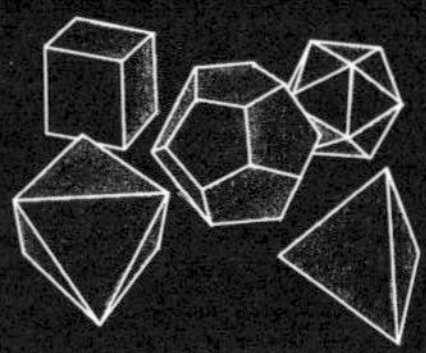

RESPONDIT, UTERQUE ALTERO INDIGET: MEDIOCRE ENIM PROPOSITUM EST PRAECETIS.

the son: father, which is nobler,
heaven or earth?
He(rmes) answered, each needs the other and we
teach to seek the middle.

Septus Tractatus Aureus

SEEING WITH TWO EYES

BY WAY OF AN INTRODUCTION

Plato, in his *Symposium*, relates a conversation between the priestess philosopher Diotima and Socrates:

> ***Diotima: '... everything that is responsible for creating something out of nothing is a kind of poetry; and so all the creations of every craft and profession are themselves a kind of poetry, and everyone who practices a craft is a poet.'***
> ***Socrates: 'True.'***[22]

Our word *poetry* comes from the Greek *poiesis,* meaning to make or compose. It is any kind of activity that makes something appear where once was nothing. The term for those doing *poesis* is *poietes* – literally, "maker" or "doer," and it is used mainly for poets who, for the Greeks, were writers of metrical verse set to music. Therefore, composition is a good word to use to translate *poesis*. Hellenistic and Byzantine Greek refers to alchemy as *chrysopoiea* and *argyopoiea*, gold-composition or silver-composition, respectively[23]. What is implied is that there are rules of composition, just as in metrical verse, for the composition of gold or any matter or substance, and that there are elements just as there are in poetry.

We are images of the intellectual essences, but statues of the unknown symbols. *Proclus. On the Chaldean Oracles. p127.*

No truth in the common assertion that evil is inherent in matter qua matter, since matter too has a share in the cosmos, in beauty and form. *Dionysus the Aeropagite. Divine Names. p120.*

According to natural philosophy from the ancient Greeks to the 17th century, all matter is composed of the four elements; Fire, Air, Water, and Earth. And all creation, the beginning, enduring, and the decaying of everything, comes from the interplay of elements and the larger phenomena to which they give rise. The theory posits that a thing can be resolved into its component elements or principles, and then recombined. In fact, you can effect a transmutation from one thing into some-

22 Plato. Symposium 205bc.

23 The Greeks also referred to it as *khemeia* to fuse, as we see in Diocletian's edict to burn the books on chemistry. With the addition of the Arabic definitive article we get al-khemia, alchemy. For a discussion of the origins of the word see, Robert James Forbes. *Studies in Ancient Technology*. (Leiden, Netherlands: E.J. Brill, 1964) 126.

You should tune the inward lyre and adjust it to the divine musician. *Corpus Hermeticum XVIII.5.*

thing quite different. This is the very essence of alchemy, and the basis for a profound consideration of being. And right here, we feel a tension between two poles: one a material process involving matter, tools, etc, and the other a quest for meaning, for wisdom.

Lovers progress from sensible to abstract to authentic beauty *Plato. Symposium. 211B-D*

The 15th century alchemist Petrus Bonus, in his *New Pearl of Great Price*, says that the philosophers "did not affect the Art for the sake of the acquisition of gold and silver, but on account of its beauty and the insight into things of the spiritual world."[24]

When 'the eye of the soul' is blinded and corrupted by other concerns, mathematics alone can revive and awaken the soul again to the vision of being, can turn her from images to realities and from darkness to the light of intellect, can (in short) release her from the cave, where she is held prisoner by matter and by concerns incident to generation, so that she may aspire to bodiless and partless being. *Proclus. A Commentary on the First Book of Euclid's Elements. p17.*

Almost paradoxically, alchemy uses the "body" to free the "spirit" through their union and their subsequent elevation toward "perfection." Alchemy, in a very concrete and material way, uses and draws from all the arts and sciences towards this end. It uses the interactions of the physical world of creation to frame the questions, "how is this world, of what is it composed, what is the nature of being."

Music, mathematics, all the arts and sciences – in short, any means of creation, could be used as well to discover and work with the inner harmonies and compositions of the world. The alchemical view is that through the discovery, awakening, and subsequent assimilation of these harmonies one is able to approach a unity of being.

From the objects of sense perception pass over now to those sights which are perceived by the mind. Behold the great order and immaterial splendor of the heavenly bodies. When thou hast seen the beauties of these, lift up thy mind beyond and noting the resplendent glory and great joy of angels do not here after be led astray with respect to the material transformation of this earthly substance, of that which is sought after with the hand and revealed by the philosophy of making gold.

***Stephanos* from Praxis Eight**[25]

The cosmos works
By harmony of
tensions
Like the lyre and
the bow. *Heraclitus. Frag 56*

Before it gave itself to the body, the soul heard the divine harmony. *Iamblichus. On The Mysteries. III.9.120.*

24 Petrus Bonus. *The New Pearl of Great Price.* (New York: Arno, 1974) 135.

25 *Stephanos of Alexandria Œcumenical philosopher and master of the great and Sacred Art. Upon Gold-making.* Trans. C.A. Browne. (C.A. Browne Papers Mss Col 418 NYCPL). All further quotes from Stephanos will be from this un-

The material practice isn't just a metaphor for the raising of the soul. Both are reflections of each other, each illuminates and explains the other. Any art form, or language of questioning, elucidates this relationship in its own way. Consider, for example, music and its metaphors of "uplift," etc. As we all know music isn't just a metaphor, there is an actual practice and theory behind making music. The theory is perhaps scant as to why or how music actually stimulates and activates the sense of uplift or any emotion, but practice makes it so through discovery and invention.

And harmonies unheard in sound create the harmonies we hear and wake the Soul to the consciousness of beauty, showing it the one essence in another kind *Plotinus. Enneads. I.6.3.*

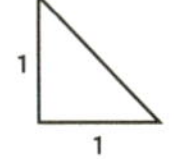

If one used music "alchemically," the "composition" wouldn't be for the sake of fame or fortune, but in order to explore the beauty and insight into all possible worlds. It would be used as a means to, and expression of, the unity of being. And through this we come to another way of knowing.

Alchemy takes these ways of knowing and takes matter, form, technique, and turns it towards gnosis, towards wisdom. Here one creates in order to know not unlike the creation of the macrocosm.

> ***For what is philosophy but the resemblance, so far as possible, of man to God.***[26]

One aspect of creation is duality. In the *Emerald Tablet*, it is expressed as the duality of the Sun and Moon, the two great lights of the macrocosm and the two great lights of the microcosm, which for discussion I will refer to as "reason" and "sur-reason." I will use "reason" as shorthand for logic, verbal, analysis, science. "Sur-reason" points to what is outside of reason. It complements reason, it includes intuition, visual knowing, poeisis/synthesis, ways of knowing beyond reason.

Mathematics, though beginning with reminders from the outside world, ends with the ideas that it has within; it is awakened to activity by the lower realities, but its destination is the higher being of forms.... It unfolds and traverses the immaterial cosmos of ideas, now moving from first principles to conclusions, now proceeding in the opposite direction, now advancing from what it already knows to what it seeks to know, and again referring its results back to the principles that are prior to knowledge. *Proclus. A Commentary on the First Book of Euclid's Elements p16.*

One way of knowing beyond reason for example, is how we can know something visually. We can correctly estimate the volume of things in order to pack them into a defined space. We never have to take a measurement. We can visualize picking up the objects and rotating them in our mind's eye to mentally work out

published partial translation of *On The Great and Sacred Art of Making Gold.*

26 Ibid.

The discovery of this (geometry) and the other sciences had its origin in necessity, since everything in the world of generation proceeds from imperfection to perfection. Thus they would naturally pass from sense-perception to calculation, and from calculation to reason. *Proclus. A Commentary on the First Book of Euclid's Elements p52*

the fit. It is a visceral knowledge built up from experience. We never have to "reason" out anything, there is no use of logic, and nothing verbal. But yet we know it will or will not fit.

Sur-reason is not the same as the irrational. By my definition, the irrational is the opposite of reason and sur-reason. The irrational is more a question of awareness than a mode of knowing and being. It is blind, ignorant of its own source and effect. Unaware, it often leads to superstition.[27] That is, we project our own noise (fears, anxieties, and desires) onto empty phenomenon, then objectify, reify, and energize it, in a system of symbolic relationships and interactions (i.e., superstitions, neurosis, etc.). This colorful morass leads to nowhere except the satisfaction of its own self-created needs. By contrast, reason and sur-reason can lead to wisdom.

Effective union certainly never takes place without knowledge, but nevertheless it is not identical with it. *Iamblichus. On The Mysteries. II.11.98*

Full union is only possible with fully developed entities – there is no unity without duality, without each aspect distinctly defined and articulated.

> ***Invert nature and you will find that which you seek. ... Combine together, says Maria, the male and the female, and you will find that which you seek. ...***[28]

The sounds which the lyre gives are an assemblage of dissonances and consonances: it is from contraries that the unity is born, which makes of the lyre, as of the universe, a well-ordered whole. *Synesios. On Dreams by Saint Synesios. p5.*

> ***Jesus said to them, "When you make the two one, and when you make the inside like the outside and the outside like the inside, and the above like the below, and when you make the male and the female one and the same, so that the male not be male nor the female female; and when you fashion eyes in the place of an eye, and a hand in place of a hand, and a foot in place of a foot, and a likeness in place of a likeness; then will you enter the kingdom."***
>
> **Gospel of Thomas**[29]

27 Keep in mind however, that sometimes superstitions hint at a deeper truth. For example, medieval talismans show traces of their hermetic past.

28 Raphael Patai. *The Jewish Alchemists.* (Princeton, N.J.: Princeton UP, 1994) 63. Maria the Jewess, Maria the Prophetess was an alchemist of 1st century Alexandria. She is truly the mother of alchemy, and invented much of the basic laboratory equipment we use today.

29 James M Robinson, ed. *Nag Hammadi Library.* (San Francisco: Harper, 1990) 129.

These two views describe the same process of union. One description from the 1st century is alchemical. Even though the language flows around the idea of transformation, it still is attached to a physical process. The saying of Jesus from the Gospel of Thomas reflects a spiritual union, but yet the language is the same, describing a process that is the same. Again we see, as in the *Emerald Tablet*, a parallel between an alchemical text and a gnostic text. It is again seeing with two eyes.

Consequently, it is evident that one discovers what is potential by performing an operation. The reason is that knowing is an act. *Aristotle. Metaphysics Book Theta (IX) 1051a*

Alchemical practice actively engages both "outer" physical processes and "inner" practices such as meditation, visualization, and dream work. It is not a question of "either/or," but "both/and." This unity is like the experience of seeing a stereographic image: each image of the pair is a fair representation of the world. However, no explanation can convey the startling experience of 3D perception when the images are fused in our mind. And with this union, we gain an insight more than either of the two images alone could provide. They mutually need each other and we need to seek the middle.

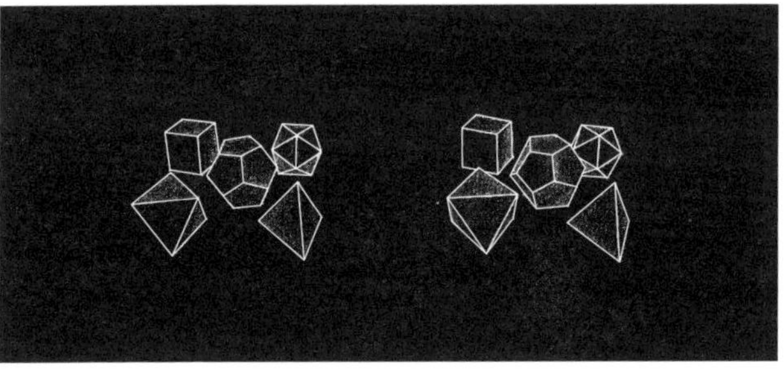

The loss of two becoming one in a third.

How to view stereographic images

With the image directly in front of you

- Place your index finger in the center between the two images
- Look at your finger tip
- Keeping your gaze on the tip slowly lift your finger towards your nose
- As it approaches your nose allow the two images to effortlessly come together

The images will appear as a 3D object floating about 9 inches from your nose

- Circle your finger around the image to strengthen the effect.
- Be patient, it may take a few attempts before the effect is seen.

The purpose of the alchemical work, the initial work, is to reclaim both views. It is not a search only for material substance, but an attempt to unite both views.

Working with both "inner" and "outer" engenders a process of discovery and invention that informs the work. And the resulting union of inner and outer is manifested in the end result, whatever form it may take, or how ephemeral it may be.

O you who seek the path leading to the secret Turn back, for it is in you that the entire secret is found. *Ibn al-'Arabī. The Meccan Revelations. Vol II p43.*

The alchemical understanding of being is that there are no hard boundaries; that it is a spectrum of awareness from ignorance to wisdom. The same "scientific" approach of testing and verification is applied to the inner realm of alchemy. The "rules" of the inner world are the same as the physical world. Oaks come from acorns, lion cubs from lions. We can't plant corn and expect oats. In other words, our actions create results like, or similar to, the actions we undertake.

Know that whoever sows wheat only harvests wheat, and if you sow wheat you do not harvest barley. Cultivate gold and you will harvest gold...

Zosimos. Muṣḥaf as-Ṣuwar. The Book of Pictures. p358

In the practice of alchemy, regardless of the *prima materia,* all aspects of inquiry, not just logic alone, all inputs, all processors must be engaged – logic, reason, intuition, myth, poetry, mathematics, ecstatcy, etc. The qualities in one mode may be invisible in another mode. Consider, for example, how images of stellar objects made at various wavelengths of the electromagnetic spectrum yield dramatically different results. What is invisible to one mode is visible to another, all revealing aspects of the world to be unified.

What is our course, what the manner of our flight? This is not a journey for the feet, the feet bring us only from land to land; nor need you think of coach or ship to carry you away; all this order of things you must set aside and refuse to see: you must close your eyes and call instead upon another vision which is to be waked within you, a vision, the birthright of all, which few turn to use.

Plotinus (I.6.8), 54.

and so...

i asked
the stones
and
the stones
answered . . .

LOVE OF WISDOM IS LOVE OF EROS

Plato. Symposium. 211B-D.

Empedocles says: 'Nothing that is has a nature, But only mixing and parting of the mixed, and nature is but a name given them by men.'
***Aristotle*. Metaphysics. Book V, Part 4.**

The ways of describing the composition of the world are many and differ in their resolution. That is, how fine grained and detailed are their respective frameworks, as well as the kinds of tools used in their observations and descriptions. Today's cosmology and the cosmology of the Greeks both hold that there are fundamental elements – building blocks – to the cosmos. Today we identify over 108 elements, but supporting those are the atomic particles and beneath these, the sub-atomic particles. As mentioned above, the Greeks considered there to be four great elements: *Fire, Air, Earth,* and *Water*, five when you add *Space*. These are respectively the principles and embodiments of energy, motility, solidity, fluidity, and the place in which it all happens.

Fire

Air

Water

Earth

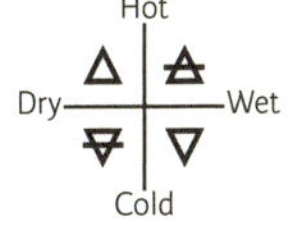

Fire lives the death of air, And air lives the death of fire; Water lives the death of earth, Earth that of water. *Heraclitus. Fragment 25*

Fire – Ares

Water – Kronos

Earth – Hades

Air – Dionysus

The four elements themselves arise from the binary oppositions of two qualities, Hot–Cold and Dry–Wet.

The philosopher Empedocles identified four great elements, *Fire, Air, Water*, and *Earth*. He also included the dynamic elements *Love* and *Strife* to capture the forces of attraction and repulsion seen operating in the world. It is through *Love* and *Strife* that the union of opposites occurs.

Two made one are never one. Arguing the same we disagree. Singing together we compete. We choose each other to be one and from the one both soon diverge. *Heraclitus. Fragment 59*

From the Four Great Elements and the Two Dynamic Elements, all other matter arises: the stuff we encounter in our day-to-day world.[30] Alchemy's focus is on the natural world, and in its development, it described and categorized metals and minerals. The first division is into *bodies* and *spirits*. Simply put, *bodies* are those things unaffected by fire, and *spirits* are those things that evaporate by fire.

30 For a more detailed explanation see Cotnoir. *Alchemy*. 24–35.

It (mercury) is made when cinnabar mixed with vinegar is ground in a copper vessel with a pestle made of copper. *Theophrastus. On Stones, paragraph 60.*

The Bodies are the metals. Classically these are gold, silver, copper, iron, tin, lead, and mercury. Mercury is counted among the bodies because it behaves like the molten states of the other bodies.

Mercury is a transitional and unstable character considered to be the root or seed of all the bodies.

Democritus called substances the four bodies, – by which he meant copper, iron, tin and lead. Everyone uses them in making the two tinctures. All substances were considered among the Egyptians as being formed from lead alone; as it is from lead that the other three bodies are derived. *Zosimos. Concerning The Question Of What is Substance And What is Non-substance according to the Art. Berthelot. III. XVII. Section 1. CAB 2 pages B5F4.*

Gold and **silver** were considered aspects of the great lights of the heavens – the Sun and Moon – the most noble of the bodies.

The remaining four bodies are copper, iron, tin, and lead. Each represent one of the Great Elements and the remaining planets:

Copper – Water – Venus;

Iron – Fire – Mars;

Tin – Air – Jupiter;

Lead – Earth – Saturn.

Copper 4: Iron 1: Lead 4: Tin 1 *Zosimos. Muṣhaf as-Ṣuwar. The Book of Pictures. p272.*

An alloy made of the four elements is called *tetrasoma* (four body), and, in Alexandrian alchemy, is a *prima materia,* the starting material.

The Spirits are the four volatile compounds that are used to act on the bodies directly by imparting a color, or indirectly to open the metals for further work.

The four volatiles are mercury, sulphur, arsenic, and sal ammoniac.

Mercury. It should be of no real surprise to find Mercury in both categories. When it is heated it flies off, vaporizes, a characteristic of *spirits.* Mercury whitens metals or is used to soften metals through amalgamation.

Sulphur. The yellow element we today call sulfur, was used directly to interact with the metals to open them up and indirectly in the dissolution and coloring of the tetrasoma through the Sulphur/Divine Water.

Arsenic, or more accurately its sulfide, As_2S_3, is the basis of the work with arsenic and its oxidation products sometimes called: "white arsenic," "white lead/ceruse" or "white sulphur," that is, As_2O_3. It is used to impart a silvery appearance to metals.

Early in our spiritual life, we heard the stones glorifying God and invoking His name. *Ibn 'Arabī Futuhat I p382. The Meccan Revelations. Vol. II. p27.*

Sal ammoniac, ammonium chloride, is used to open up and volatilize the body.

The remaining minerals and prepared compounds of the natural world are further divided and categorized into salts, vitriols, etc. The compilation of these "lists of stones," starts with Theophrastus, student of Aristotle, and continues on through the Byzantine lexicons and the works of al-Rāzī and al-Khawarizmī, for example.[31]

This is the starting point. It is with these materials and the various methods such as calcination, distillation, ceration,[32] etc. that matter is moved from station to station. The four elements, and more specifically, the two principles underlying the elements, were the guide in understanding how various forms of matter would interact. Early medicine provides a clear example of the theory in practice.

31 See for example the following works: John F. Richards. *Theophrastus on Stones*. Columbus, Ohio: Ohio State U, 1956. The Byzantine *Lexicon of the Names of Minerals Used in the Divine and Sacred Art*. in Berthelot, M. *CAAG* Vol 1. French p 3–18, Greek p 3–17. Al-Rāzī's *Al-Madkhal al-Ta'līmī* and his *Kitāb al-Asrār the Book of Secrets* as well as Al-Khawarizmī's *Mafātih al-'ulūm* are found in *Chemistry in Iraq and Persia in the 10th Century AD*. Memoirs of the Asiatic Society of Bengal. Vol VIII, No 6. H.F. Stapelton, R.F.Azo, Hidaya Husein. P 317–48. Jābir ibn Hayyān's *Book of Stones* is to be found in Haq, Syed. *Names, Natures, and Things*. Kluwer Academic Publishers. Dorchester, Netherlands. 1994.

32 Ceration – making wax-like. It is a point in the work where and when the volatile and the fixed are joined, initially making the material in question wax-like.

Yellow Bile
Fire *hot & dry*

Blood
Air *hot & wet*

Phlegm
Water *cold & wet*

Black Bile
Earth *cold & dry*

Health, as defined in Hippocrates elemental theory, is the harmonious interplay of the four elements expressed in the human body as the *humors*. Health was maintained or restored by balancing the humors or elements with compounded drugs that would augment or suppress the humors in question.

Democritus was right. Thus you should know that the whole work can only take place in the case that you know each thing in particular; it is only then that you know the method whereby it is necessary to proceed to the mixture, according to the weights which are appropriate to ensure the perfect execution of it. It is necessary therefore that the philosopher knows everything before putting his hand to the work, if the thing is, or is not, of what thing it is made and how it is." *The Book of Cratés. p35*

The Greek physician Galen (30–100 CE) developed a system for determining the strength of substances and their composition into drugs that was widely used in one form or another through to the 17th century.

The worlds are four: the highest world, which is the world of subsistence; then the world of transmutation, which is the world of annihilation; then the world of inhabitation, which is the world of subsistence and annihilation; then the world of relations. These worlds are in two locations: the Greater World, which is everything outside man, and the Smaller World, which is man. *Ibn al-'Arabī. The Origin of Creation. 120.27. The Meccan Revelations. Vol 1 p38.*

In Galen's system of drug composition[33] not only are the elements considered, but also the deeper more fundamental level of the properties – Hot–Cold, Wet–Dry. He divided each property into five degrees, one temperate and four of intensity. The degrees are based on the intensity of the effect determined by the body's reaction to them. Starting at neutral with Temperate, these are things that have no effect on the body. The degrees then follow increasing in intensity. The First degree is the mildest, almost imperceptible. The Second degree has a visible effect, the Third degree has a strong one, and the Fourth degree is extremely potent. It is corroding, even lethal.

Diagnosis of the patient would indicate the composition of the drug, a *pharmakon,*[34] to make up the missing elements: to strengthen the weak, and to bring balance to the humors via the combined properties of the composition. The preparation is not a simple mixing but, according to ibn Sīna, a "fermentation" that needed to take place to change it into its own entity. This involves various methods of cooking, digestion, etc. Through this "fermentation," the original materials are destroyed and a new one arises with new potencies (properties) that have the desired effect of re-balancing the humors, thereby restoring health. The parallel with the alchemical process

33 Galen. *De Complexionibus* and *De simplici medicina*. For full discussion see Michael McVaugh. *Arnald de Villanova Opera Medica Omnia II Aphorismi de Gradibus*. Universidad de Barcelona. Granada- Barcelona. 1975.

34 *Pharmakon*, is generally a powder.

of composing an elixir[35] is striking. Like the medicinal composition, an alchemical elixir is a composition that will balance by adding any of the four elements or their qualities that are missing from the matter in question, and so bring it to perfection, to its completion. Here Democritus uses the language of medicine to describe how one proceeds in the work.

Do not be surprised at the notion of an incorporeal structure, for it is like the structure of a word. *Corpus Hermeticum. XI.17.*

...students of physicians who want to prepare a beneficial drug do not set about making it on a rash impulse, but first of all they test which kind of drug is hot; which kind, when joined to it, produces a balanced mixture; which kind is cold or wet; and of which kind is the affection, whether it is appropriate for the balanced mixture.[36]

Later Jābir ibn Hayyān (721/722–815) developed theories of matter based on language and a system of balances. Based on the analysis of the objects name in Arabic, deeper patterns and its composition in terms of the four qualities: dry, wet, hot, and cold emerge. By the values of the letters the degrees of each quality can be determined. Once it is properly analyzed, what it needs to balance and perfect the matter at hand can be worked out.[37]

Make the corporeal incorporeal and the incorporeal corporeal. *Hermes III. IV. Berthelot. Vol 2. 124.*

د	ط	ب
ج	ه	ز
ح	ا	و

And Maria said about the making of lead-copper "take drugs!" By that she meant the rust which is the smashed sediment, and the exalted stone which has its nature in it. *Zosimos. Muṣhaf as-Ṣuwar. The Book of Pictures. p204*

You should know that the root is one, one matter, one substance and from it the art is one and is accomplished with it...[38]

The alchemical work begins with one thing, "one matter," the *prima materia*, i.e. the tetrasoma (the alloy made from lead, copper, tin, and iron) is formed. An alternative, *molyb-*

35 Elixir is derived from the Greek word *xerion* a medicinal drug. In Arabic it becomes *al-iksīr* to eventually become *elixir.* Originally thought of as a drug to restore balance to a specific imbalance, it evolved over time to mean a universal elixir that can cure any imbalance. Alchemy calls this the Philosopher's Stone, which is not a stone but, like the original Greek *xerion*, a powder.

36 Martelli, Matteo. *The Four Books of Pseudo-Democritus. Sources of Alchemy and Chemistry.* Ambix Vol. 60, Supp. 1. (Leeds. 2013) 97.

37 See Sayed Nomunal Haq. *Names, Natures and Things.* (Kluwer Academic Publishers. 1994).

38 Morienus. 1974. 12f.

But when the spirit of darkness and of foul odor is rejected, so that no stench and no shadow of darkness appear, then the body is clothed with light and the soul and spirit rejoice because darkness has fled from the body. [...] Maria: 'Lead, copper, dissolve both of them equally.' *Zosimos. Muṣhaf as-Ṣuwar. The Book of Pictures. p298.*

dochalkon – made only of lead and copper, was developed by Maria the Prophetess and was continued in the work of Zosimos. Zosimos clarifies further:

Darkness no longer has dominion over the body since it is a subject of light and they will not suffer separation again for eternity. And the soul rejoices in her home, because after the body had been hidden in darkness, she found it filled with light, and she united with it, since it had become divine towards her, and it is now her home. For it had put on the right of divinity and darkness has departed from it. *Book of Komarios IV.xx. 15.*

Mary alone has proclaimed that among these writers she spoke with reference to all substances when she says, 'Whenever I speak of copper or lead or iron I mean their rust.'[39]

In making the alloy, the metals aren't used, but rather the salts of the metals as we see in Democritus'[40] *Physika kai mystika*:

Take white earth – I mean the earth composed by white lead,[41] ***[...] You shall whiten it by crushing it in seawater, or brine, or rainwater – I mean under the dew and in the sun – so that after being ground it turns as white as lead. Then melt this and add to it copper flower or the rust that has been scraped off***[42] ***[...] until it becomes solid and unperforable, it will become easily so. This is the molybdochalkon.***[43]

The prima materia is fused and worked into a thin wafer or leaf. The leaf is placed into the upper chamber of the kerotakis. The divine water, *theon hudor*,[44] is placed in the lower chamber called Hades. Zosimus refers to this as the "divine water" or "the bile of the serpent." A deep reddish-yellow liquid made by boiling flowers of sulphur[45] with slaked lime.[46] The recipe from the Leyden Papyrus (4th century CE) for the "Water of Sulphur,"[47] reads:

39 Berthelot. Vol 2. III.XVIII. Greek, 170. French, 169. Translation from the Greek by C. A. Browne. Folder B5 F4. "Concerning The Question Of What The Art Has Said About All Substances With Reference To A Single Tincture."

40 (circa 300 BCE)

41 PbO

42 CuO. In addition to the quoted sources of copper "rust" azurite a copper carbonate is mentioned.

43 Martelli. 93.

44 Θείου ὕδωρ – Water of Sulfur. Θείου ὕδατος – Water of the Divine. Θείου means both sulfur and divine. See Robert Halleux. *Papyrus de Leyde. - Papyrus de Stockholm. - Recettes.* (Paris: Les Belles Lettres, 1982) 104.

45 Sublimated sulphur.

46 Calcium oxide.

47 The term *Sulphur water* meant other solutions as well. Careful consideration of the context is needed to determine which material is being specified. Sulphur water, in addition to being a calcium sulphide, was either, depend-

Silver in cold sulphur water turns pale to deep gold color.

Silver in hot sulphur water turns deep matte black.

Lime, one drachme; sulfur previously ground, and equal quantity. Put together in a receptacle. Add some sharp vinegar or urine from a virgin boy, heat from below until the added liquid looks like blood. Filter because of the sediment. Use pure.[48]

This is heated and the spirits rise and work on the prima materia. Zosimos quotes Maria:

The various colored efflorescences of bodies signify the fulfillment of what has been well carried out in their interior. *Stephanos of Alexandria. Upon Gold-making. Sixth Praxis.*

If the two do not become one – that is, if the volatile are not combined with the fixed, nothing expected will take place. If you do not whiten and the two do not become three, with white sulphur, which whitens, nothing will take place which is expected.

The appearance of beauty are signs of an invisible loveliness. *St. Dionysus. Celestial Heirarchies*

But when you yellow, three becomes four, for you yellow with yellow sulphur.
Finally when one tints into violet, all the materials join together in unity/Violet.[49]

It appears that in all of the processes involving the kerotakis the color progression of the stages is the same. The matter worked on goes from black, white, red/yellow, to violet/purple. Again and again we find reference to this color sequence in the texts. Not only in Alexandrian alchemy, but in European alchemy as well, because as alchemy spread and developed, this basic color sequence, determined from the physical practice and material results, became an essential symbol along with the many other symbols that came with it. And over time, place, and practice, the colors, sequence, and their matter and meanings shift.[50] The substances used in the kerotakis process may vary from process to process, and we must understand that

If your vision of it (monad) is sharp and you understand it with the eyes of your heart, believe me, child, you shall discover the road that leads above or, rather, the image itself will show you the way. *Corpus hermeticum IV.4.11.*

ing on the text, mercury and its compounds, arsenic and its compounds, or antimony and its compounds.

48 Halleux. 104. Also in Berthelot. 46-47. Calcium sulfide is the result of this process. It is also known as sulfurated lime, calcic liver of sulphur, liver of lime, and hepar clacis.

49 Zosimos. *On The Body of Magnesia and On its Treatment*. III, XXVIII, 9. Berthelot. Vol 2, 192.

50 The color sequence in Western alchemy includes a rainbow, iridescent shift through a range of colors often symbolized by the peacock. This may suggest a shift in the prima materia and or the process.

All of these things are one, and one work. They differed about the names, but the work is one. *Zosimos. Muṣhaf as-Ṣuwar. The Book of Pictures. p294*

this work is a dialogue with matter, as all experiment is. But at the core of it is the meaning of change. In the process a small amount of gold or silver acts as a fermenting agent like yeast. According to alchemical theory, it is the color that performs this role. Each result is to be treated with a higher substance. So that lead or tin is fermented by molybdochalkon, copper is fermented by silver, silver by gold and gold is fermented by "coral of gold". And for the Hellenistic alchemists to change the color is to change the metal. The degree of excellence is one of color. Zosimos, quoting Maria the Jewess, reminds us:

> ***...Do not think that she meant that it would turn into silver like the silver of ordinary people, nor that it would turn into gold, like the gold of ordinary people, but she (Maria) meant with it the colors.***[51]

Know that copper only turns black if it is mixed with gold and silver, and it can only have shiny exalted colors appearing on it when it is composed. *Zosimos. Muṣhaf as-Ṣuwar. The Book of Pictures. p315*

The color of the material is the name of the stage: Melanosis, Black; Leukosis, white; Xanthosis, yellow/red; and Iosis, purple.

***Melanosis*, Black.** The first color change occurs as the prima materia decomposes. "Do not be discouraged because of your inexperience, said Zosimos, for when you see that the metal has turned to cinder, understand that everything is going well."[52] The heated fumes of the *Divine Water* turns the leaf black and slowly decomposes it. Some texts seem to suggest that the fallen decomposed material in the *Hades* and the remaining decomposed black matter still on the foil are put together, dried to a powder, ground, mixed, and then fused in preparation for the next stage. This is generally depicted by images of decomposition, death, decay, dismemberment, and, in the chain of metaphors, anything associated with this breakdown, such as the raven, or coffin, etc. ***Leukosis*, White.** The second change occurs as the prima materia is purified of its corruption much like the disruptive, chaotic, disgusting decomposition of a corpse ends with the whitening of the bones. The shadows have been removed and it becomes white like silver. When the

Democritus: 'Take the mercury from cinnabar' because what is extracted from the cinnabar is the only one which makes the copper white and makes its shadow disappear and it makes it red in the second work.' *Zosimos. Muṣhaf as-Ṣuwar. The Book of Pictures. p420*

51 Zosimos. *Muṣhaf as-Ṣuwar. The Book of Pictures* (Living Human Heritage Publications, 2007) 363.

52 Olympiodorus. *On The Sacred Art*. Berthelot. *CAAG* Vol 1. 107.

prima materia is whitened, it is whitened on the outside but is yellow on the inside indicating that the alloy is evolving into gold. In this stage, the alloy is fused with a small amount of silver as ferment. It is then exposed to *Divine Water* either by immersion or exposed to fumes in the kerotakis by circulation. With exposure, the prima materia becomes silvery white like silver.[53] Washing, bathing, water images in general, such as the swan are typical of the imagery used to express this state/station. ***Xanthosis,* Yellow/Red.** This is the ripening of the prima materia, after it is broken down washed and whitened, it is primed for color, where the forces unleashed through its purification now evolves to its final state. In this particular kerotakis process, the prima materia is fused with a small amount of gold and it is exposed to fumes of *Divine Water* for the yellowing. The inside and the outside are now yellow.[54] The prima materia has now taken on a new color and is re-born. The phoenix is a perfect image for this stage as is any image of resurrection, rebirth, renewal etc. Even though the prima materia has reached its perfection, there is a final stage of projection. ***Iosis,* Violet.** *Ios* of Gold[55] (*ios* of violet). The final stage imparts penetration, color, and projection. This powder, also know as the powder of projection becomes known in European alchemy as the philosopher's stone. The *Book of Komarios* states: "Lastly the production of rust (or violet) is a putrefaction, it is a putrefaction of the species of things, that is to say production of rust (or violet) and putrefaction are the final transformation of the composition for the coloration of gold."[56] *Ios* can mean rust, virus, violet and poison. And when considering its qualities, all these meanings are correct: it is

This light is one and the same in its entirety everywhere, is present indivisibly to all things that are capable of participating in it, and has filled everything with its perfect power; by virtue of its unlimited causal superiority it brings to completion all things within itself. *Iamblichus. On The Mysteries (I.9.31)*

Enlightened by the knowledge of what we have seen, we shall then be able to be consecrated and consecrators of this mysterious understanding. Formed of light, initiates in theurgy, we shall be perfected and bring about perfection." *Dionysus the Aeropagite. Ecclesiastical Hierarchy 372B*

53 There are other whitenings, for instance, that start with copper and either mercury or arsenic both of which can, under proper conditions, give a silver appearance to copper through arsenic or mercury adhering to the surface. Always the particular materials called for all depend on the whole of the process. The same names can be used to refer to several things depending on the context.

54 If mercury was used in the whitening, when the sulphur water/divine water is boiled and the sulphur fumes, the sublimated sulphur joins with the mercury on the surface of the alloy, the mercury and sulphur combine to form the brilliant red of mercury sulfide.

55 Ios of copper = red sub-oxide, green basic carbonate, Ios of iron = red iron oxide, venetian red,

56 *Book of Komarios* IV. XX. Section 6. Translated by C. A. Browne. Berthelot. *CAAG* Vol 3. 278.

"Now when anything else comes to perfection we see that it produces, and does not endure to remain by itself, but makes something else." *Plotinus. Ennead V.4.1*

a rust in that a very fine powder forms; it is a spiritual color, very concentrated, almost free of the body; a virus in that it spreads or replicates itself; violet for that is its color; and it is a poison in how it permeates and transforms all bodies for that is it's strength.

> ***But our gold which posses the desired quality can make gold and tint into gold. Here is the great masterpiece – that the quality becomes gold and it then makes gold.***[57] **Zosimos**

Although we are stirred to activity by sense objects, we project the ideas within us, which are images of things other than themselves; and by their means we understand sensible things of which they are paradigms and intelligible and divine things of which they are likenesses. As these ideas within us unfold, they reveal the forms of the gods and uniform boundaries of the universe." *Proclus. A Commentary on the First Book of Euclid's Elements p112*

The general protocol for the work is that first, lead and copper is fused and then decomposed by way of the kerotakis and divine water. This decomposed mass is the Black stage result. This Black stage result is mixed and fused. Silver is added to the alloy and decomposed by way of the kerotakis and divine water. It is then worked producing silver. This is the White stage and this silver, "our Silver," is the end result. This White stage result is fused with gold. It too is decomposed through the kerotakis and divine water, then fused and processed. This is the Red Stage and this gold, "our Gold," is the end result.

Considering this I noticed the parallel between this process and that of Corinthian silver and gold, or what is now called depletion gilding. "Formerly a mixture was made of copper fused with gold and silver, and the workmanship in this metal was considered even more valuable than the material itself"[58] writes Pliny in his *Natural* History, further speaking of Corinthian bronze he says that:

> ***There are three kinds of this sort of bronze: a white variety, coming very near to silver in brilliance, in which the alloy of silver predominates; a second kind, in which the yellow quality of gold predominates, and a third kind in which all the metals were blended in equal proportions.***[59]

57 Zosimos quoted in Maurice Crosland. *Historical Studies in the Language of Chemistry*. (Mineloa, NY: DoverPhoenix, 1978) 54.

58 Pliny. *Natural History, Vol. 5*. Trans. H. Rackham. (Cambridge: Harvard UP, 1999) 129.

59 Pliny. 133.

Briefly, the process for gold is rather straightforward. Approximately 65% copper, 10% silver and 25% gold are fused together. It is then pickled and cold worked.[60] This cycle of pickling and cold working is continued until the acid eats away the copper and silver, leaving only gold on the surface. Following a similar process using 85% copper and 15% silver, a silver surface is produced. Both the kerotakis process and Corinthian processes use the same metals in similar proportions. Both use mineral salts[61] and acids to dissolve copper etc. Both cold work, hammer and pound, both go through the same color progression.

But Latona for her intrigue with Zeus was hunted by Hera over the whole earth, till she came to Delos and brought forth first Artemis, by the help of whose midwifery she afterwards gave birth to Apollo. *Apollodoros. Library 1. 1.4. Loeb p25.*

This process follows the texts. Where it stops is at the creation of the violet – a purple powder of projection. The name *iosis*, "purple rust," suggests a surface formation on the metal, an actual rust. If we understand this to be a violet or purple powder the making of which involves gold, there is a pigment that is exactly this. Known as the Purple of Cassius, after Andreas Cassius, it is a purple pigment made from gold. The recipe was published in 1685 by his son of the same name in his book *De Auro*. However, it was known before then that certain gold compounds can give a red color to glass and glazes. It is however speculation that this final stage is the making of this powdered purple pigment.

Aqua regia
2 parts *Aqua fortis*
1 part *spirit of salt.*

Take some of the glass and set it on a gentle fire. If you see its color starts to become purply-black, do not fragment it even once, otherwise it will not come out good. *Zosimos. Muṣhaf as-Ṣuwar. The Book of Pictures. p512.*

Glauber in *Des Teutschlandts Wohlfahrt* (Latin *Prosperitatis Germaniae*) 1656–60 first describes precipitating gold from an aqua regia solution with a tin compound.

> ***Take of the Calx of Gold 1 lot (or half ounce) and dissolve it in three or four lots of strong rectified Spirit of Salt: Pour unto the Solution twelve or fifteen Lots of pure water upon all this, put two Lots of Tin, and set the Glass that the Solution is in, upon hot Sand, and heat it scalding-hot, but let it not boil. When it hath thus stood for one or two hours, all the Gold will be turned into Powder, of a Purple and Gold—like hue, and settle to the bottom. Then***

60 Copiapite, salt, vinegar or urine

61 These are generally sulphates and chlorides this is discussed in a later chapter.

Gold Stannate
CAS Registry Number: 1345-24-0
Additional Names: Aurous stannate; C.I. Pigment Red 109; C.I. 77482; gold-tin precipitate; gold-tin purple; purple of Cassius. Colour Index Vol 4 (Yorkshire: Society, 1971) 4669.

having poured out the Water, and separated the Tin, separate all the Acrimony from the Powder by several washings, and so will you have it fitted for the Confection."[62]

When you place this powder on copper and heat the copper, it turns gold. Keep in mind that you are working with symbols. Transmutation gives metallic body to volatile substances that is color. When the volatile has taken on a bodily form, that is, when the metal has taken on color, transmutation has taken place.

Purple of Cassius Recipe #1
Solution 1. Gold Solution. 0.5gr of gold is dissolved in 27.0 gr aqua regia (16.8gr HCl and10.2 gr HNO_3) diluted with 14 liters of water. ***Solution 2.*** Tin chloride solution. 3gr of finely divided tin dissolved in 18gr of aqua regia with additional 5ml of water.***Solution 2 (tin)*** is added drop by drop to the Gold solution. The precipitate of the purple oxide is washed with boiling water. The purple precipitate at red heat turns a brick-red color.

Recipe #2
Dissolve gold in Aqua regia. Dissolve tin in aqua regia Add gold solution to some water. Add ½ the amount of tin solution to gold solution Purple precipitates out.

Recipe #3 Glauber 1 part Calx of Gold 1 part HCl 12–15 parts Water 2 parts Tin.

Recipe #4
The process by which the finest purple is obtained is, according to Fuchs, to add stannous chloride to a solution of ferric chloride until the yellow colour is changed to a pale green, and then to precipitate the gold solution with this mixture. *Roscoe. A Treatise On Chemistry. London: Macmiilan, 1890. p588*

The process is based on this or something like this. But it isn't so much the techna of it, as what the praxis reflected or helped elucidate, that is, one's relation to creation and the move toward unity of being.

As the final stage it is not only complete, perfected, but can, and whose role it is, bring other things to perfection, to completion.

In the writings of Zosimos, he speaks of an actual physical process, a laboratory protocol, if you will, as well as an initiatic aspect, an inner, more "spiritual" aspect. When asked by Theosebia his mystical sister, why the sages disguised their works with difficult names and examples, Zosimos answered that if the work "would be made visible, the world would become corrupt, and the work would become something like glass-making."[63]

Here he is implying another dimension to the work: a more initiatic, meditative process with more than just gold making in mind. It seems as if the main concern here is the ascent of the soul through the development of visualization

62 J.R. Glauber. *Des Teutschlandts Wohlfahrt Part IV.* (Amsterdam, 1656-61) 35-36. English translation. *Prosperity of Germany Part 4.* (RAMS edition) 330-331.
63 Zosimos. 2007. 145.

and meditative practices associated with, or embodied in practical physical work. And in the work's perfection, the perfection of the artist is expressed. As Plotinus observes, "For the beautiful and the real beings certainly do not come from the bad, or from things indifferent. For the maker is better than what is made, because more complete."[64]

Lovers progress from sensible to abstract to authentic beauty. *Diotima. Plato Symposium 211B-D.*

64 Plotinus. Enneads. V.5.13.197.

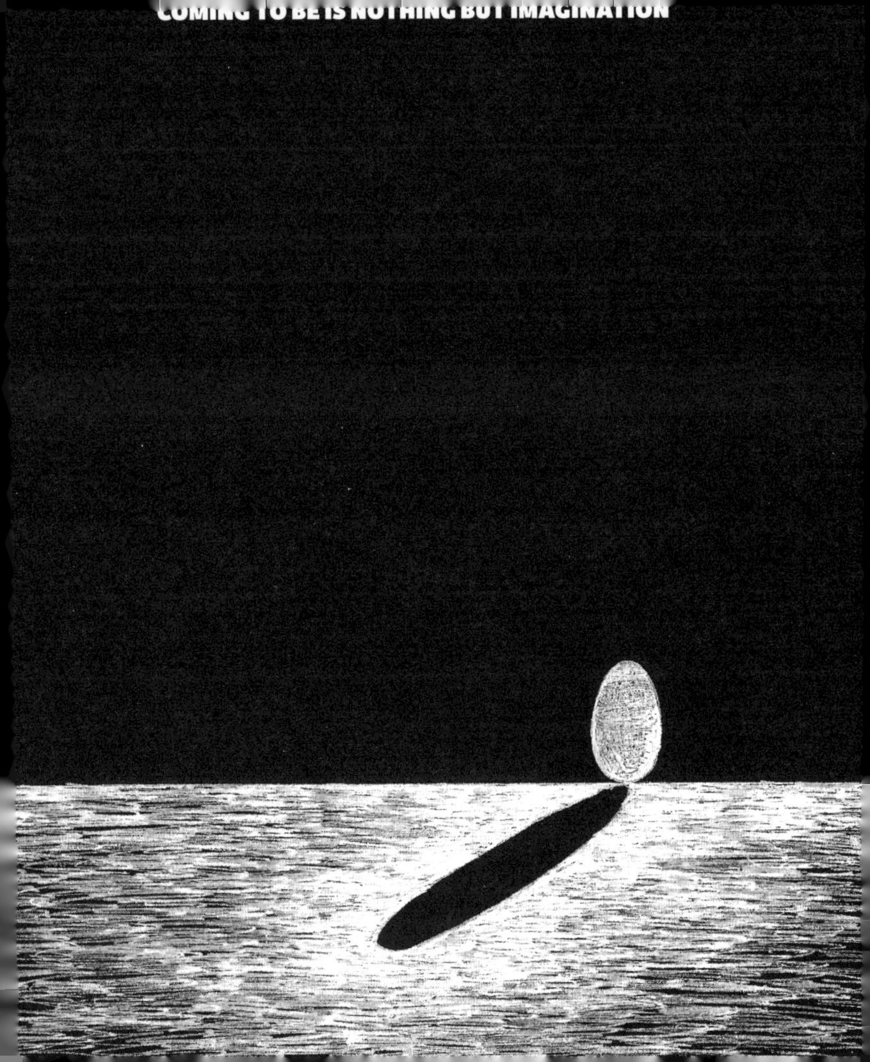
COMING TO BE IS NOTHING BUT IMAGINATION

Corpus Hermeticum V.1.

"ALL TEEMS WITH SYMBOL."

PLOTINUS ENNEAD III.2

The way of alchemy is to enter into matter, into the symbol, into the object, and to open it up, turning the gaze inward to the other side of the symbol. This is *theoria.* It is a kind of seeing, a consideration with the minds eye that goes beyond speech.[65] It is not just a spatial seeing, or a compositional seeing. *Theoria* while gazing outwardly, points inward toward the sources of creation it grasps the emptiness, so to speak, from which creations arise. And so it, itself arises.

Here the impossible actually takes place. *Faust Part II. Goethe*

At the intersection of microcosm and macrocosm, in the encounter between mind and matter, between "in here" and "out there," symbols arise. Symbols reveal, join, and share in the two worlds. They are grasped whole in a flash. The two worlds press into each other, and the boundary, like the film of a bubble, is pinched off and named. All of creation and all created things are symbols. It is an ongoing self-disclosure, and any phenomenon is its expression and explication.

Yet all things follow from the word. *Heraclitus. Fragment 1*

In our interaction with the world discrimination comes first, then naming. Discrimination is that moment when an event is grasped by the mind, when boundaries are thrown up around a phenomenon when something is marked as separate or distinct from its surroundings. It is the "tangible" intermediary between the material world and the immaterial.

The human soul being on the boundary line between corporeal and incorporeal substances, and dwelling as it were on the horizon of eternity and time, it approaches the highest by receding from the lowest. *St. Thomas Aquinas, Summa Contra Gentiles II c.81.*

Along with this discernment after the boundary, an image, a name, an icon arises from this. When you see something and name it, you have symbolized it. Even if it is just a description – "that round thing over there," a sound or visual image arises with this bounded object, and it is symbolized – given a name. Not that a name is in and of itself a symbol, the name is the end result of the symbolizing process. Every object is thus a symbol, part of which is its name.

Thus the bodiless are reflected in bodies, and the bodies in the bodiless, that is to say, the physical world is reflected in the mental, and the mental in the physical. *Corpus Hermeticum. XVII.*

65 It is from here that our word "theory" is derived but has not the same meaning at all. *Theoria* is not a theory or a conceptual framework.

Imagination is the first body of the soul. *Synesius. On Dreams p9*

Here is a thought experiment, or a meditation, however you wish to think of it, on how to open up an object and explore its borders and its creation.

First, read through this process then actually do it.

Object

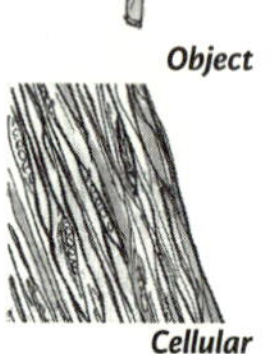

Cellular

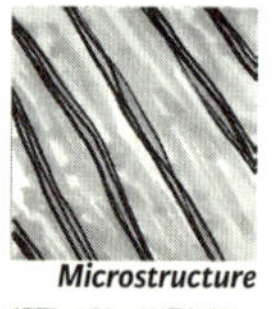

Microstructure

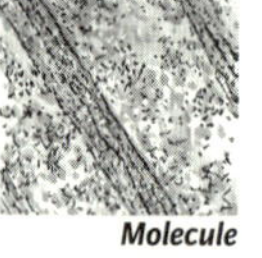

Molecule

The sequence imagined here, using contemporary physical models, is a series of magnifications from the physical surface appearance of an entity, here a "wooden chair," through its gross structures, compounds, molecules, atoms, sub-atomic particles, etc. to it's "final" energy gradient. Using this model of the "wooden chair" as a guide to the stages, select an object that is in view when you look up from the page. Now enter into this object to see what is there. In your mind's eye, zoom in as it were, to a very close-up view of the object and the surrounding air. In your mind's eye you can see the details of the wood, the grain and knots, etc. Zoom in even closer to the cellular level and note the microstructures. Choose a part and go in closer still to the molecular level. Zoom into the atomic level, and space is mostly what you see. Keep going down to the sub-atomic "particles." It is pure energy, and any differences are very subtle energy gradients. Let the visualization develop and let it stabilize. Strengthen it by cycling through it several times.

Then on the last cycle

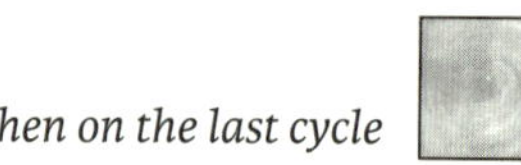

lift your eyes and look

at the object just analyzed.

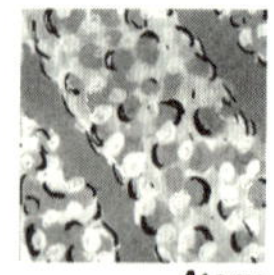

Atoms

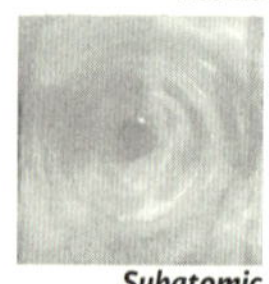

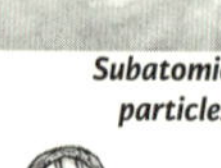

Subatomic particles

The moment in which the absence of qualities changes to the establishment of an identity, is the moment of discrimination, of naming, the moment of symbolization.

CHAIR

I have noticed that when I do this, that there is sense of a projection in the giving of names – the projection through our eyes, or any of our senses for that matter, of our mind piecing together and forming borders.

Perhaps the medieval theory of vision was trying to understand and explain this process of symbolizing and naming. This theory held that vision was due to a projection of a ray from the eye to the object – a projection "illuminating" the object. Although vision is now understood to be light rays reflecting off of an object entering the eye, I would like to reconsider the first theory in a more non-materialist way by looking at it through the experience of the above meditation. That is, when we perceive, we have a sense of projection onto empty objects – forms, ideas, definitions etc. in the naming/discriminating process. And this projection comes from us as we form images of the world out of our present and past experiences.

This intersection between the macro and microcosm, has been called the *mesocosm*, the symbolic realm of poetry, of dreams, of alchemy. It is in this boundary world where all may take place. Here, in this isthmus, thin as the breath, a symbol may reveal its "meaning," and show us a way to the shore of an endless ocean.

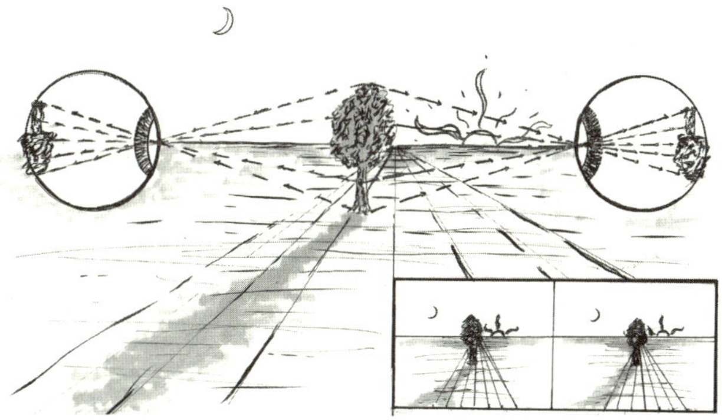

Trace the creation back through our eyes – where does the boundary lie?

On the microcosm side of the isthmus, each phenomenon arises from the face of the infinite as we press against our world. And each finite fragment is an entry point to the infinite. Alchemy – an image of the worlds reflected in each other – arising from each other with each other – the heavens reflected in the earth and the earth in the heavens. To descend into earth, into matter is to enter into the heavenly realms.

Consider this image from the manuscript *Splendor Solis.*[66] A two-headed winged hermaphrodite (union of sun and moon, king and queen) holds an image of the Aristotelian sublunary cosmos in its right hand and an egg in the left hand.

The image of the cosmos depicts the four elements. Earth is in the center, with Water the wide white band surrounding it. Then Air, with the outer most band representing Fire.

The egg also symbolizes the four elements unified into a fifth, or *quint*-essence, representing the result of the cycle of creation. It also represents the beginning point (a chicken is an egg's way of making another egg). Here we see an image of the worlds reflected in each other.

The Fifth Similitude of the *Splendor Solis* (1532–1535), which is the text accompanying this image, is about the four elements and the quintessence.

To show this in a parable, the philosophers describe an egg in which four things are conjoined. The first, outermost one is the shell – the earth – and the white is water. But the skin between the water and the shell is air, and it divides the earth from water. The yolk is fire; has around it a subtle membrane which is the subtle air. That which is in the innermost part is the subtlest, for it is nearer the fire, and separates fire and water. In the middle of the yolk is the fifth (essence), out of which the young chick comes forth and grows.[67]

66 Karl R. H. Frick. *Schatzkammer der Alchymie*. Hamburg 1718. (Akademische Druck-u. Verlagsanstalt, Graz. 1976) Fifth Similitude 183.

67 Salomon Trismosin. *Splendor Solis.* Trans. Joscelyn Godwin. (Grand Rapids: Phanes Press, 1991) 38.

From the Fourth Dictum of The *Turba Philosophorum* (9th century CE)

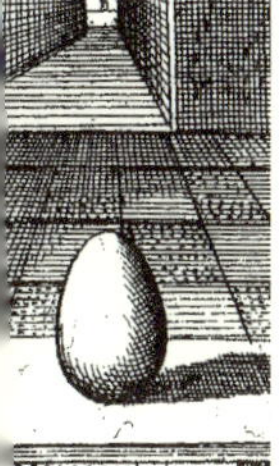

An egg is an illustration, for therein four things are conjoined; the visible cortex or shell represents the earth, and the albumen, for white part, is the water; the yolk also of the egg represents fire; the cortex which contains the yolk corresponds to that other air which separates the water from the fire... In the egg, therefore, are four things – earth, water, air, and fire.[68]

Continuing on into the heart of Fire lies the sphere of the Moon within this: Venus; on through to Saturn and beyond the Stars.... The Egg and The Cosmos are the inverse of each other; the material world is but the thin and porous border between the two. A journey up and outward is the same as the journey down and inward. We come to the same boundary from perhaps seemingly opposite directions. The alchemical approach takes the matter at hand as the starting point and sees it as the symbol that it is.

Lunar Magic Square

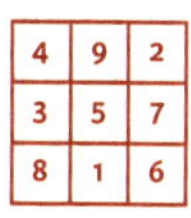

4	9	2
3	5	7
8	1	6

Girolamo Cardano. *Practica aritmetice et mensurandi singularis*, 1539.

Cracking the Egg, we enter...

De-territorialization – breakdown of categories and boundaries, or perhaps not so much a breakdown but an opening up, more porous and fluid (even crystalline). Opening to the very last apparent boundary, it is no longer material but conceptual like the boundary between salt and fresh water.

The way up and the way down is one and the same. *Heraclitus Fragment 60*

This is the doorway to a symbol, a doorway from the visible to the invisible. It is that moment, that opening in time, where transmutation becomes possible. Slow this down, open it up, hold it steady and examine it.

The first act of governance of Saturn is destroying and bringing to light *Plato. Rosarium Philosophorum*

68 A.E. Waite. *Turba Philosophorum*. (New York:Weiser, 1970) 11.

... if someone wants to, let him descend to the generative soul and right on to what it makes, and then ascend from there, from the ultimate forms to the forms which are ultimate in the opposite sense, or, rather, to the primary forms. *Plotinus. Ennead V.3.9.*

The shell of the microcosm, the material earthy crust of creation of the macrocosm, the thin film of foam between the macro and the micro is penetrated.

Alchemy is a material symbolic process of ascent through the descent into and through matter. This image of descent before the ascent has its roots perhaps with shamanism. It is a journey taken in many myths. The story of Orpheus is one that comes to mind. Another comes from the story of Christ's resurrection in the "apostles creed" where it is stated that Christ "descended into Hell and on the third day rose again." And consider Dante's *La divina commedia.* It starts the evening before Good Friday and begins with his descent into Hell before the ascent through Purgatory to Paradise.

Nothing, however, is corruptible or destroyed – terms that disturb human beings. Life is not birth but awareness, and change is forgetting, not death. *Corpus Hermeticum. XII.18.*

She (the soul) wants to penetrate within herself to see the circle and the triangle there, all things without parts and all in one another, to become one with what she sees and enfold their plurality" *Plato. Phaedrus. p113*

The first stage in this descent begins with a dislocation, an ecstasy, a death, or a dream. In alchemy, this initial stage is spoken of in most violent terms and depicted in images of dismemberment, a shattering of the form that holds the "soul" – that "it" that needs to be free to live. It has been compared to a person trapped in the rubble of an earthquake who is being pulled from the wreckage, cutting and breaking them in the process – alive, however. Psychologically speaking, it is that nauseating, stomach dropping sensation as you realize all is collapsing around you, as a thousand realities tear apart the unified fantasy of the so-called real world.

Like this, is the first dissolution.

Saying these things I went to sleep, and I saw a sacrificing priest standing before me at the top of an altar in the form of a bowl. This altar had 15 steps leading up to it. Then the priest stood up and I heard a voice from above saying to me, 'I have accomplished the descent of the 15 steps of darkness and the ascent of the steps of light and it is he who sacrifices, that renews me, casting away the coarseness of the body; and being consecrated priest by necessity, I become a spirit.' *Zosimos. On Virtue. Lesson 2.*

When it all turns to ash, know all is good.

As one descends, penetrating the earth and form, the shell, the crystalline form ruled by Saturn is entered – Kronos the boundary is crossed. There are symbolic equivalencies at play here, circling around the ideas of Earth, Saturn, shell, surfaces, structures, and boundaries. Consider once again the structure of the cosmos; in Cicero's *The Dream of Scipio* Africanus says to his grandson Scipio, "Below the Moon there is nothing except what is mortal and doomed to decay, save only the souls given to the human race by the bounty of the gods, while above the Moon all things are eternal."[69] But the Moon itself? It is the border between the material and the divine in a fluid ever shifting play of light and form. It is that realm of dream where symbols arise. And it is here in dream, the lunar realm of alchemy, that transformations first appear.

Earth is the Moon
Water is Mercury
Air is Venus
Fire is the Sun
Fire is Mars
Air is Jupiter
Earth is Saturn
Pico della Mirandola. Heptaplus.

The sage said it has nine letters composed of four parts, and that the first three parts have two letters each. *Zosimos. Muṣhaf as-Ṣuwar. The Book of Pictures. p279.*

Our way through the boundary, the shell, is found in the play of symbols, imagining the process through the sliding of images. And we soon discover that there is a dream element within form that becomes more apparent and clear as the form opens through the process. Start with Saturn and you will discover Saturn has an inner Lunar quality. Enter Saturn via the Moon and so begin to open the body. This is the descent via the Saturnal-Lunar realm of dream.

69 Cicero. *The Republic*. VI. *The Dream of Scipio*. Translated by Clinton Keyes. (Cambridge: Harvard UP, 2006) 270–271.

They declared that the immutable part of the universe extended from the outer sphere, which is called aplanes, the fixed sphere, down to the beginning of the moon's sphere, and the changeable part extended from the moon to the earth. *Macrobius. Commentary on the Dream of Scipio p131*

This form of dream is not so concerned about the content of the dream but the awareness of the "mechanism," the underlying state of consciousness that supports the dream. There is a very strong tendency to be drawn into the displays and dramas of the dream world as in this world, but, most importantly, one should make all attempts to look behind the curtain. Look to the consciousness, the awareness that is supporting these displays. Awaken within the dream. It is good to read the letters but it is imperative that you find their source.

Whoever descends into Hades uninitiated and unpurified shall grovel in the mire; but he who has been purified and initiated shall on his arrival there dwell with the gods. *Iamblichus. The Exhortation to Philosophy. p65-66.*

Alchemy takes place in both the waking physical world and the shifting realm of dream. These realms are not opposites of each other, but symbols of the same process. Work with both to awaken to the consciousness underlying the two. The process has an affect not as subject on object, but as something in existence out of a series of relationships. Every change in object implies a change in the subject; reciprocity is not a cause and effect but an outgrowth of the relationships amongst all the bits that compose whatever "thing" in the world we are considering. Remember that it is the child that creates the parents. A parent arises with the birth of a child.

Hecate: Execute my statue, purifying it as I shall instruct you. *Chaldean Oracle 224*

In between the two, the immortal and the mortal, the circling moon. *Corpus Hermeticum. XI.7.*

Let this be our understanding, for the present, of the intermediate status of mathematical genera and species, as lying between absolutely indivisible realities and the divisible things that come to be in the world of matter. *Proclus A Commentary on the First Book of Euclid's Elements. p4.*

Theosebia asked: "'How can I see a vision, while I am awake?' He (Zosimos) said: 'although your eyes are looking, your heart and your understanding are sleeping. When your understanding gives help, and your eyes see, then you will see the truth. But if your understanding does not help, then they are normal dreams.' She said: 'I do not understand what this is.' He said: 'I have told you the truth. So sharpen your eyesight, wake up your mind, and empty your thoughts.'" [70]

70 Zosimos. 2007. 331.

How do we break through these symbols, how do we soften the boundaries, or, alchemically speaking how do we open the body? How do we enter into the shut palace of the King and so effect a transmutation from the imbalanced and impure to the beautiful, full of virtues?

Bereave matter of its substance in order that it may pass over to a spiritual state, which is the accomplishment of our final purpose. The aim of philosophy is the dissolution of the body and the separation of the soul from the body.

Stephanos of Alexandria.
On The Great and Sacred Art of Gold Making. ***Fourth Praxis.***

To begin we must open up and sink into and through the body, to follow the labyrinth, the folds to the center, to open and reveal the light, through the body by transfiguration. And after transfiguration, transmutation is possible, where noise becomes music.

To Hekate
Lovely Hekate of the roads,
and of the cross-roads I invoke.
In heaven, on earth,
then in the sea, saffron-cloaked,
tomb spirit reveling
in the souls of the dead,
daughter of Perses, haunting deserted places,
delighting in deer, nocturnal,
dog-loving, monstrous queen,
devouring wild beasts,
ungirt and repulsive.
Herder of bulls, queen and mistress of the whole world, leader,
nymph, mountain-roaming nurturer
of youths, maiden, I beseech you to come to these holy rites,
ever with joyous heart, ever favoring the oxherd.
Orphic Hymns. Translated A. Athanassakis and B. Wolkow.

We must turn our power of apprehension inwards, and make it attend to what is there. It is as if someone was expecting to hear a voice which he wanted to hear and withdraw from other sounds and roused his power of hearing to catch what, when it comes, is the best of all sounds which can be heard. *Plotinus. Enneads V.1.12*

Make yourself grow to immeasurable immensity, outleap all body, outstrip all time, become eternity and you will understand god. [...] Go higher than every height and lower than every depth. Collect in yourself all the sensations of what has been made, of fire and water, dry and wet; be everywhere at once, on land, in the sea, beyond death." *Corpus Hermeticum. XI.20.*

YOU SHOULD KNOW

THAT THE ROOT IS ONE,

ONE MATTER, ONE SUBSTANCE

AND FROM IT

THE ART IS ONE AND

IS ACCOMPLISHED WITH IT

Morienus

Here at the boundary, taking matter, we observe and manipulate it in our hands, in our minds, in our hearts. Alchemy, working with matter, is an active meditation on creation, the aim of which is the ascent of the soul; from concrete to abstract to authentic beauty.

Let us become fire *Proclus. On the Chaldean Oracles p124*

Zosimos says:

> ***This work is of two types: one of them is a hidden thing that the sages kept secret for the intelligent people in order that they might extract it by their contemplation and precise understanding. As for the second type, it is delusions and vanities, made from many operations and many things which are all false.***[71]

Stephanos, in his *On The Great and Sacred Art of Making Gold* (617 CE) amplifies this idea:

> ***Mythical chemistry is one thing, and the mystical and hidden is another. For the mythical chemistry is confounded in a multitude of words, but the mystical is operated by the word of the Creator of the world, that the man who is holy and born of God may learn by the direct operation and by theological and mystical words.***[72]

Very early on, alchemy distinguished between two kinds of alchemy, or what he calls "chemistry." There is the *mythic* "confounded in a multitude of words," a multiplicity of words, lost in the noise. And there is the *mystic* which deals with the universe through deliberation on the creation and its method consists in images (symbols). And it is this mystic way, in the direct operation and mystical words that we have, as Stephanos calls it, the "way of the philosopher." He explains further:

The method of mystical chemistry consists of (celestial/heavenly) images and whatever is necessary is accomplished by method. *Stephanos of Alexandria. On The Great and Sacred Art of Making Gold.*

71 Zosimos. 2007. 358.
72 Stephanos of Alexandria. *On The Great and Sacred Art of Making Gold.* (C.A. Browne Papers Mss Col 418 NYCPL.)

For a person of this kind, being fond of contemplation and understanding matters of nature, examines closely into the theories of all things; he carefully investigates all their natures, compounds their union according to rule, resolves intelligently both their associations and ten thousand compositions, accomplishes with skill the combination that has been mentioned and focuses his general observation upon simple unity. He will have a plain knowledge in these matters that is theoretically and decidedly correct.

We have three aspects to the method. The first aspect is the engagement of both hands on work, direct operation, along with theological and mystical words. This is expressed later in Western alchemy in the concept of *laboratorio* and *oratorio*, the laboratory and the prayer room.

The second aspect is the use of celestial "images." In the context of Byzantine alchemy such a comment or term is to be understood as an icon, which is the link between the two worlds. The image is a manifestation, conceptual or theoretical as in *theoria*.

Having illuminated all his mind, this beauty kindles his whole soul and by means of body draws it upward, and beauty changes his whole person into essence. *Corpus Hermeticum X.6.*

The third is the use of all ways of knowing, rational and surrational and suggests that unifying the views in a "simple unity" will provide a correct view. By taking the insights of Art combined with Science and by this method, this alchemical process of seeing with two eyes, one is able to have a direct perception of reality, the *Book of Crates* says:

Thus you should know that the whole of the work can only take place in the case that you know each thing in particular: it is only then that you know the method whereby it is necessary to proceed to the mixture, according to the weights which are appropriate to ensure the perfect execution of it. It is necessary therefore that the philosopher knows everything before putting his hand to the work, if

the thing is, or is not, of what thing is it made and how it is.[73]

Zosimos states, "You have to read the books and make them part of you by experiments and reading because experiments and reading will guide you to the truth."[74]

You should know that the root is one, one matter, one substance and from it the art is one and is accomplished with it...[75]

Ænigma of The Philosophers Stone

Nine letters I have.
Four syllables am I
Understand me
The first three syllables
Each have two letters
And the remaining the rest
And the five are silent
And of the total number
The hundreds twice eight and
Thrice three tens and four.
Knowing who I am
You will be initiated
In the divine wisdom
That I contain.
M. Berthelot. Collection des Anciens Alchimistes Grecs. Vol. III. 267.

Here Morienus, a "student" of Stephanos, paraphrases the *Emerald Tablet,* continuing the Hellenistic alchemical tradition in its transmission to the Arabs. The work is part of the alchemical tradition from Alexandria handed down to us through the Byzantines and Arabs, and as such, it is a summary of alchemy. The *Liber de compositione alchimiae* is the first alchemical text known to be translated into Latin from Arabic. It is the story of the meeting of Morienus, a Christian monk who had succeeded in the work of making the elixir, the powder of projection;[76] and Khālid ibn Yazīd, an historical figure who had supported the arts and sciences, including alchemy. The conversation between the "Hermit" and the "King" gives the whole of the process, and we see many of the images, concepts, and processes that will thread their way through the development of alchemy in the West. In a sense, the practice of alchemy has been a thousand year meditation on this work of Morienus and Khālid.

73 *Book of Cratès*. Trans. and Intro. Adam McLean. (Glasgow: Hermetic Research Series, 2002) 35.
74 Zosimus. 2007. 285.
75 Morienus. *A Testament of Alchemy. Being the Revelations of Morienus to Khālid Ibn Yazīd*. (Hanover: The Brandeis UP, 1974) 12. This is a translation of *Liber de compositione alchimiae*. The *Liber de compositione alchimiae* was translated from Arabic into Latin. The original Arabic manuscript is entitled *Risālāt Mariyanus al-Rāhib al-Hakīm li-l-amīr Khālid ibn Yazīd, The Epistle of Maryanus the Monk, the Wise to Amir Khālid ibn Yazīd*. MSS Fatih 3227 (fol. 8b-18b) and Sehit Ali Pasha 1749 (fol. 61a-74b). Istanbul.
76 This is the end result of the Opus Magnum, the Great Work and it has the power to effect transmutations. The powder of projection is often described as a powder red or violet in color.

Throughout the text, Morienus gives clear indications as to the materials. When Khālid asked Morienus to explain the terms he used, Morienus replied: "Before I explain them to you, I will bring before you the things called by these names, that you may see them, as well as work with them in your presence."[77]

> ***...if you wish to seek, distribute, and dissolve them, and stiffen and join, and confect them exactly as I am about to do before you, you have but to do likewise,***[78] ***for this is the root of this knowledge and operation,...***
> ***...one who by means of his knowledge discovers this composition will easily understand the entire operation...***[79]

Morienus says that by questioning the material, the way forward will be become clear as the nature and qualities become known to you. To put the materials or possible materials in context, here are only some of the substances, a palette, so to speak, of what was available to work with. Essentially these are any and all products and by-products of the world. Alchemy, as mentioned earlier, focuses mostly on minerals and metals and divides them into broad categories such as: **Bodies** that are stable when exposed to fire, such as Gold, Silver, Iron, Copper, Lead, Tin, and sometimes Mercury; **Spirits** that fly when exposed to fire – Sulphur, Arsenic, Mercury, and Sal ammoniac. There are also all the **Minerals** and **Salts**, such as marcasite, malachite, turquoise, lapis lazuli borax, vitriols, magnesium, zinc, talc, kohl, water of iron,[80] lodestone; and **Artificial** substances, the end results of certain processes, as well as side products to be used in other operations, for example verdigris, vermillion, dross of metals, white lead, red lead, tuttia or zinc oxide.

And some of the key operations in alchemy are distillation, calcination, lixivation, circulation, sublimation, solution, coagulation, ceration, and amalgamation.

77 Morienus. 1974. 39.

78 When Morienus states, "you have but to do likewise," he is also establishing an essential aspect of science, that is, repeatability.

79 Morienus. 1974. 31.

80 This is a water made from extinguishing red hot iron in water. The water was then used. This seems to be the basis for an early aurum potabile. See page 150, 'Wine of Extinguished Gold.'

What Morienus is saying is take these materials, use these processes, create and change the world. This is alchemy. The way is in the matter itself, for whatever else alchemy may be, it is a physical practice based on available materials. Some may have fantastic names but there is no fantasy about them, they are actual minerals and other salts. The question always is, what do these names point to, what do they mean?

> ***Morienus spoke: The things in which the entire accomplishment of this operation consists are the red vapor, the yellow vapor, the white vapor, the green lion, red ocher, the impurities of the dead and of the stones, blood, eudica and foul earth.***

Gather the materials and put them before you.

From these things, Morienus states, you can create the elixir. Whereas Khālid had Morienus showing him the materials at hand, putting names to substance, we have to attempt to identify what these are and how they are used. By using the way of the philosopher, I will start with the Green Lion for no other reason than that it is an image that has circulated throughout alchemy.

I am not attempting to give an exhaustive survey here of the Green Lion's appearance in alchemy, but enough to both illustrate the way of the philosopher, and the nature, substance, and function of the Green Lion.

So then, what is the "matter" of the Green Lion? In short, the Green Lion is known by its function. So the question "is this it, is this 'thing' before me the Green Lion?" must be answered by seeing if the substance in question has the function as defined by the protocol of the Opus Magnum.

With many paths to the same end, it follows that perhaps there are as many Green Lions as there are paths. The material or process that the term "Green Lion" symbolizes or "points to" may vary depending on the path followed, but would perform a similar function in each case. Much in the same way that the object we call a "key" serves the same function (to lock or unlock) regardless of the material composition of the "key" and "lock." The material that makes up the "key" will differ depending on the nature of the lock. The "key" could be made of metal, wood, a plastic card with a magnetic strip or even a series of numbers. In the same way, the Green Lion may be copper; malachite (dehnegi); green vitriol, iron sulphate, $FeSO_4$-$7H_2O$; Qalqand, a mix of $CuSO_4$ and $FeSO_4$; it is Oil of Vitriol, sulphuric acid (H_2SO_4); Aqua Regia, (HCl/HNO_3 mixture); Salt of Saturn, lead acetate, $Pb(CH_3OO)_2$; antimony acetate, $Sb(CH_3OO)_3$; stibnite, the raw ore of antimony; regulus of antimony, pure antimony (Sb); mercury (Hg); or the philosophical mercury itself, amongst other things.

The things in which the entire accomplishment of this operation consists are the red vapor, the yellow vapor, the white vapor, the green lion, red ocher, the impurities of the dead and of the stones, blood, eudica and foul earth. *Morienus. 39.*

This exploration, or perhaps more accurately – this meditation, will be somewhat ahistorical. By looking at the symbol or image across time and culture we find, from time to time, a more luminous center within the symbol. Viewing a symbol in this way, while at the same time neither ignoring the actual context in which each of these images, metaphors, or symbols occurs, nor forgetting its physical aspects, and attempting to view it as an integral whole, we come to a more profound understanding of the matter at hand, in this case, the Green Lion.

This list most likely signifies, respectively:
- red orpiment,
- yellow sulphur,
- quicksilver,
- green vitriol,
- red earth/latten,
- lead/tutia,
- orpiment,
- glaze vitreous mineral,
- sulphur.

So we start with Morienus, and the work that first introduced the Green Lion to the Latin world. According to the *Liber de Compositione alchimiae*, the Green Lion is one of the ten things that go into the Great Work.

leo viridis est vitrum,
the green lion is glass.

In defining the Green Lion as glass, Morienus is saying that it is vitriol. We can see this in the Latin terms *vitriolum* – vitriol and *vitreum* – glass[81] that *vitriol* derives from *vitreum*. There is a similar Arabic pairing in the main manuscript of *Kitāb Ḥall ar-Rumūz*[82] by Muhammad Ibn Umail, it reads, "...they named their water... the water of vitriol." In two other manuscripts[83] of the work in question, the term "vitriol," in Arabic, "*zāj*," is replaced with the term "glass," "*zujāj*."

Another example of a switched term is in the *Turba Philosophorum*.[84] In some manuscripts of the *Turba Philosophorum*, the term "green lion" is substituted with the term "green stone." I think it is rather clear that what is being spoken about, at least in the texts that were translated from Arabic into Latin, is green vitriol, an iron vitriol or even a copper-iron vitriol.

There is also another kind of verdigris called from the Greek worm-like verdigris, made by grinding up in a mortar of true cyprian copper with a pestle of the same metal equal weights of alum and salt or soda with the very strongest white vinegar. This preparation is only made on the very hottest days of the year, about the rising of the Dogstar. The mixture is ground up until it becomes of a green colour and shrivels into what looks like a cluster of small worms, whence its name. *Pliny. Natural History Book XXXIV. Chapter XXVIII. 116.*

Vitriol refers to a class of compounds that today we call a sulphate. In the past, the compounds were also called *atraments* for its use in tanning leather (after the Greek term for shoemaker's black – *atramentum*).

Vitriol was also used in producing acids, the "sharp waters," or "the oils" that can dissolve metallic bodies. The "sharp waters," such as aqua fortis (nitric acid is able to dissolve all metals except gold) and aqua regia (a nitric and hydrochloric acid mix is able to dissolve all metals including gold), were produced using vitriol as an ingredient. Vitriol itself produced "oil of vitriol" or, as it is called today, sulphuric acid, which can dissolve all metals except silver and gold. Later vitriol comes to mean any acid. Its use in metalworking is mentioned by Pliny the Elder (CE 23 – 79). In his *Natural History*, Book XXXI, he describes a mixture including *misy*, either an iron sulphide or iron sulphate used in the cleansing of gold. Vitriol was also an ingredient in the

81 George Crabb. *Universal Technological Dictionary* (1833), "vitriolum (*chem.*) from *vitreum*, glass, on account of its resemblance to glass."

82 Ibn Umail, Muhammad. *Book of the Explanation of the Symbols. Kitāb Ḥall ar-Rumūz*. Theodor Abt and Wilfred Madelung eds. (Zurich: Living Human Heritage Pub, 2003) 61.

83 A) Tehran manuscript Malik library Tehran, Iran MS 3187. B) Astan-e Quds Library. Meshhed, Iran MS 10763. See above note. Muhammad Ibn Umail.

84 Waite. *Turba* Philosophorum. (New York: Weiser, 1970) 67. Twentieth Dictum "Certain wise men have designated it after one fashion, namely, according to the place where it is generated; others have adopted another, founded upon its colour, some of whom have termed it the Green Stone..." according to Waite, "the second recension reads: Green Lion."

making of Corinthian gold, a bronze and gold alloy used in the arts.[85] Essentially, it is made by forming a copper and gold alloy. The surface of the alloy is then pickled with the use of vitriols which dissolve the other metals leaving only gold at the surface. It is then cold worked and burnished (see page 87).

The physician alchemist Al-Rāzī (900 CE) lists six vitriols in his "Classification of Minerals."[86] They are green vitriol (iron sulphate, FeSO4-7H2o, melanterite); blue vitriol (copper sulphate, CuSO4-5H2O, chalcanthite); white vitriol (zinc sulphate, ZnSO4·7H2O, goslarite) and alum (potassium aluminum sulphate KAlSO4, alunite); calcatar (yellow or red atrament); and a green atrament called calcande (from the Arabic *qalqandis*). It is this last one, the green vitriol called *qalqandis* that interests us.

Verdigris
Los scolycos "worm-like rust"
Copper mortar and pestle
+½ Hemina of strong white vinegar (2 parts) and urine (1 part)
+4 drachme Alum
+4 drachme Sea Salt
OR
+4 drachme Alum
+4 drachme Natrun
Macerate under hot sun and strong sunlight, stirring it becomes greenish and sticky, work the paste and roll into worms.
Rose-worms.
Dioscorides. De materia medica. V.79.

One reads in Galen[87] (CE 129–210) how the green vitriol salts were prepared by allowing the water run-off from copper mines to evaporate in caverns, forming the green crystals. The most common ore of copper is chalcopyrite, CuFeS, a copper-iron sulphide. When weathered, it forms a copper-iron sulphate solution, which is a green solution due to the presence of iron.

In the *Mafātih al-'Ulūm*, The Key of the Sciences, by Abu 'Abdallah Muhammad bin Yūsuf al-Kātib al-Khawarizmī written around 980 CE we read that, "qalqandun is green; on moistening it, and rubbing it on iron will turn the latter red."[88] What is being described is a green solid substance, which indicates iron sulphate, that when moistened and rubbed on a piece of iron metal, causes the iron metal to go into solution forcing the copper out of solution and depositing it on the iron metal, turning it red, which indicates the presence of copper sulphate.[89]

Copper sulphate is a blue crystal or stone which when dissolved in water gives a blue solution, while iron sulphate is

85 The Nicanor Gate in the Temple of Jerusalem is reputed to have been made of Corinthian gold.

86 H.E. Stapleton. 'Chemistry in Iraq and Persia in the 10th Century AD', *Memoirs of the Asiatic Society of Bengal (Calcutta)*, VIII, No.6, 1927. 318-441.

87 Galen. *De simplicium medicamentorum temperamentis ac facultatibus, IX.* (Kuhn ed. XII) 238-241.

88 Stapleton. 364.

89 This reaction is easily observed by immersing a clean iron nail into a solution of copper sulphate. The copper

green. When the two are mixed the green color predominates. The fact that this green stone produces copper shows that it is a mix of copper and iron sulphate. This qalqand is the most likely candidate, out of the range of salts and minerals available, to be the Green Lion of Morienus.

Grind *sōri* and copper flower together with unburnt sulphur; *sōri* looks like azurite that easily peels off and is always found in *misy*. It is also called green copper flower. Roast it at a moderate heat for three days, until it becomes a yellow drug. Lay it on the copper or on the silver that is made by us and it will become gold. *Democritus PS93 Section 13. (Berthelot Section 12)*

Although there is not any one thing that says this explicitly, when all the texts, descriptions, and physical behavior are taken together, from this linguistic haze emerges the vitriolic form of the Green Lion. It appears to be a mix of copper and iron rather than just solely iron.[90]

It is interesting to see how this idea of the union of iron and copper, of Mars and Venus, has circulated and hovered around the image and idea of the Green Lion. Here, for example, is the union as described in the 1605 edition of Joseph DuChesne's *The Practise of Chymicall and Hermetical Physicke*:[91]

> ***The same also is to be seen in Vitriol, the which among other Salts is most corporeal. For always for the most part figures and Images of Venus and Mars, are to be seen therein and conjoined together.***

Theologists surveying the causes of these things in the gods, enclose Venus and Mars, and surround them with Vulcanian bonds; the difference which is in the world being connected through harmony and friendship. *Proclus. Procl Comm. Parmen. 847, 26ff*

This blend of copper and iron has been called the Marriage or Union of Mars and Venus.[92] DuChesne continues to say that vitriol is the source of the Green Lion:

> ***In this Vitriol, I say, do plainly appear, Salt, Sulphur, and Mercurie. Whose Mercury altogether etherícall, being by art separated and made most pure, from the elementary passive flame, possess-***

comes out of solution and deposits on the nail as the iron from the nail goes into solution, giving the appearance of iron transmuting into copper. Paracelsus considered this to be a proof of the possibility of transmutation. See his *Tincture of the Philosophers* in *The Hermetic and Alchemical Writings of Paracelsus Vol 1*. Ed. A.E. Waite. (New York: University Books, 1967) 28.

90 Another possibility is a basic iron sulphite, a mineral called copiatite that is very active and aggressive toward copper.

91 Joseph Du Chesne. *The Practise of Chymicall and Hermetical Physicke.* (London, 1605) Chapter XIII.

92 The full story is told in Homer. Odysseus. Book 8. 265-310.

eth a great sharp spirit, of so great an acting and penetrating force, that in a very short time it will dissolve metaline bodies and most hard substances, whether they be metals or stones. And this is that green lyon, which Rypley commenteth so much.

Vitriol, as noted above, became a term for any acid, and the most potent of the early mineral acids is aqua regia, the king's water. It is used to open the body of gold, that is, to prepare a calx of gold that can then be used in subsequent alchemical work, whether potable gold or the Opus Magnum.

But why would or should aqua regia be considered a Green Lion? I have found no early text that identifies the Green Lion as aqua regia, but terms do shift, and the parts of something can come to signify the whole. One of the terms for an ingredient in making aqua regia (i.e. green vitriol/Green Lion) could come to give its name to the whole end product. Although no *early* text was found to bolster this idea of the Green Lion being aqua regia, towards the end of the 17th century we see that Johannes Rudolph Glauber gives his recipe for aqua regia,[93] or what he calls the Green Lion.

Sea coals or in defect of them Wood coals powdered. Salt peter, common salt and oil of vitriol. One part of each is put into a retort. Distill off all humidity. Then increase them at length and a Green liquor[94] of Sulphur will come over, which the ancients called the Green Lion, which dissolves Sol, and which they are digested a good while.[95]

The earliest mention of aqua regia is in the Arabic literature. In these texts, aqua regia is called *al-mā' al-ilāhī* (the divine water)[96] or *mā' al-ḥayāt* (the water of life), taking the name from Hellenistic alchemy.

93 One thing to note throughout all these recipes is that, wherever you see chloride salts *and* nitrate salts together, you have the ingredients for aqua regia. All that is needed is a careful distillation.

94 Sulphur compounds can impart a green color.

95 'The Secret Fire of the Philosophers.' In Johannes Rudolph Glauber. *The Works of Johannes Rudolph Glauber.* (RAMS edition) 21.

96 Perhaps a reference to the *theon hudor* – the sulphur or divine water of the Greeks

In a process that goes back to the Sixth Shi'ite Imam, Ja'far al-Sadīq (d.765), one first makes a solution of potassium nitrate, called "natrun water" in the text. Then take of this solution,

> ***one hundred* dirhams, *and throw in it ten* dirhams *of alum, ten of sal ammoniac and five* dirhams *of* qalqatar *which is* zāj *(vitriol)... After you throw the mixture in the* natrun *water leave the whole for two days and two nights and distil in a cucurbit and alembic. Take what is distilled and it will be clear and white as tears.***[97]

This is aqua regia.

From the *De inventione veritatis* the late thirteenth century translation of a text by Geber, we find a recipe for nitric acid and aqua regia:

> ***First R of Vitriol of Cyprus, lib. 1. of Salt-peter, lib. ff. and of Jamenous Allum one fourth part; extract the Water with Redness of the Alembeck (for it is very solutive) and use it before alleged Chapters. This is also made much more acute, if in it you shall dissolve a fourth part of Salammoniac, because that dissolves Gold, Sulphur, and Silver.***[98]

So, was aqua regia the Green Lion? Well, certainly in later alchemy, it was defined as such. But was aqua regia the Green Lion of Morienus? Not very likely, but with what we know of vitriol as an ingredient in early recipes for aqua regia; let us take another look at what Morienus says about the Green Lion. Later in the *Liber de Compositione alchimiae*, after we have been told that ten things are necessary for the elixir, we find another mention of the Green Lion as part of a process that calls for four ingredients.[99]

97 Julius Ruska. *Arabische Alchemisten.* (Wiesbaden: M. Sändig, 1967) 115-116. Cited in Ahmad Y. Hassan's essay "Potassium Nitrates in Arabic and Latin Sources," at www.gabarin.com/ayh/Nitrates.htm.

98 Ḥayyān, Jābir Ibn, and Richard Russel. The Alchemical Works of Geber. (York Beach, ME: S. Weiser, 1994) 223-224.

99 Morienus. 1974. 42, 43.

Morienus said: Take the white vapor, i.e. virgin's milk, and the green lion, i.e. fire, and red ocher, i.e. fire, and the impurity of the dead, i.e. earth...

If we interpret this list as the beginning of the work on the elixir, we see an intriguing possible interpretation for a list of the ingredients for aqua regia.

Taking *White Vapor* to mean sal ammoniac, one of al-Rāzī's four volatiles, sublimates as a white frost. The *Green Lion* is vitriol as shown above. Consider the *Impurity of the Dead* to be salt peter, potassium nitrate, and *Red Ochre* to be ordinary red clay. With these ingredients follow the traditional method for distilling vitriols, i.e. acids, from minerals.

The salts are moistened and mixed with the clay and rolled into small balls, they are dried and then dry distilled.

The distillate is aqua regia.

This is possible but yet, Morienus warns about understanding the meaning of alchemical texts. He says, "The ancients, however, did not refer to the matters pertaining to this science by their proper names, speaking instead, as we truly know, in circumlocutions, in order to confute fools in their evil intentions."[100]

300 years later, the English alchemist Sir George Ripley (1415–1490) in *The Bosome-Book of Sir George Ripley*, states that in fact vitriol is *not* the Green Lion.[101] In this book, which is nothing less than "the whole work of the composition of the Philosophical Stone," he gives his method of preparing the true Green Lion, thus defining it.

The two things that may be used to start the process are antimony or sericon, a salt of lead.[102] In general, the metal or the oxide of the metal is dissolved in distilled vinegar. The solution

100 Morienus. 1974. 11.
101 "Vitriall, which fooles doe call the greene Lyon." George Ripley. *The Compound of Alchemy of Sir George Ripley.* (Norwood, NJ: Orbis Terranum, 1977). 'Erronius Experiments'.
102 Sericon is minium (red lead) or litharge (a yellow lead). In the *Map-*

is then filtered and crystallized, resulting in the Salt of Antimony (antimony acetate) or the Salt of Saturn (lead acetate). This is the Green Lion of Sir George Ripley who used it as the basis for his elaboration of the Great Work.

Are any of these the real Green Lion? First let all that was said above inform this simple definition. The Green Lion is that which, through devouring gold, purifies and frees the soul of gold, thus making it available for the higher processes of alchemy involving the "elixir" or the "philosopher's stone." Whichever material it may be, that is, by definition, the Green Lion.

While it may be said that all these Green Lions discussed are valid aspects of a variety of true paths, it may also be that this variety of substances is an indication of a somewhat unsuccessful search for the "true" Green Lion. Our ancestors undoubtedly tried various formulations of the Green Lion in the hopes of making the elixir. And when one substance didn't work, they more than likely moved on to another in the hopes that it would be "it." So, perhaps when actual vitriol didn't work out in a process for the elixir, a closer look was made and it was determined that, in fact, it was not ordinary vitriol that was meant, but perhaps something that shared certain qualities, features, etc. with ordinary vitriol. So again and again we come across statements that the word vitriol refers not to ordinary vitriol, but to the "vitriol of the philosophers," or "our vitriol," which could and does represent a wide variety of substances and ideas.

When coming across this term "*x* of the philosophers," or "our *y*," recognize that in general, the use of these terms indicates that the material in question is not the ordinary x, y or z, but yet shares certain qualities, metaphors, etc. with the ordinary x, y, or z, and may be of a different matter entirely.[103] Take for example the pair "mercury" and "mercury of the philosophers." In one we recognize ordinary quicksilver, Hg, the silvery liq-

pae Clavicula of the 8th or 9th century, "siricum is made from white lead; it is also made from lead." Smith and Hawthorne. *Mappae Clavicula.* (Philadelphia: American Philosophical Society, 1974) 55, item 192-D.

103 To confuse matters further, "philosophical x" could be ordinary "x" used philosophically. That is, in the pursuit of wisdom.

uid stuff in thermometers. In the other, we have something that says it shares some of the qualities of ordinary mercury but it is not. What qualities does this have that most reminds the alchemist of quicksilver? Both are "waters that do not wet the hands" and both are volatile and are used to purify gold. This is true with the pair "vitriol" and "our vitriol," as in the case of Sir George Ripley's Green Lion. It is not ordinary vitriol, the "vitriall of fooles," but another material altogether – "our vitriol."

In continuing our search for the Green Lion, "our vitriol," we find some direction in the following emblem. This emblem appears in Basil Valentine's *Azoth*, published in Paris, 1659.[104] We see in the upper center a goblet surrounded by the symbols for the seven planets/metals. The goblet stands on Mercury with the Sun and Moon both pouring something into the goblet. The Moon is on the right and the Sun on the left, with Venus and Jupiter beneath the Moon and Saturn and Mars beneath the Sun. In the center of the emblem is a ring that is linked to two shields. The shield on the right bears a double tailed lion rampant, perhaps the Green Lion, and the shield on the left shows a double-headed eagle.[105] Linked between these two shields and hanging from them is

104 Basil Valentine. *Azoth, ou Le Moyen du Faire l'Or caché des Philosophes.* 1659. (Genova: Edition Anastatique, 1976) 146. This emblem has been associated with the *Emerald Tablet* since 1588 and was joined to the text to elucidate, or depict the teaching engraved on the *Emerald Tablet*. S. Gentile and C. Gilly. *Marsilio Ficino and the Return of Hermes Trismegistus.* (Florence: Centro Di, 1999) 205.

105 These images also represented the Holy Roman Empire whose emblem is the double headed eagle, and Bohemia with the double tailed lion. This also a third smaller shield emblazoned with a seven-pointed star. Surrounding this smaller shield are three objects. The object on top of the stellar shield is the Orb of the Earth, on the left of the shield is an armillary sphere showing the equator and the ecliptic, and the object on the right represents the heavens.

There are also hands emerging from clouds between the cluster around the goblet and the cluster around the ring. Finally, around the circumference of the emblem is inscribed the following: *Visita Interiora Terrae, Rectificando Invenies Occultum Lapidem*, which, roughly translated, means, "enter into the earth, rectify and you will find the hidden stone." The first letters of the words of the motto spell out V.I.T.R.I.O.L.

This is an emblem rich in meaning, which, with proper meditation, reveals much about alchemy and its processes. However, I will limit the scope of its examination to questions concerning the Green Lion. What is of interest here is the center shield with the star, the orb above it and the motto, all of which point to antimony, or more precisely to stibnite, an ore of antimony. The orb is the symbol for earth and for the metal antimony. The shield below displays a star, the form that highly purified antimony takes, called by the alchemists the star regulus of antimony. The motto has many levels of interpretation, one of which suggests taking earth, that is, antimony, and entering into it and purifying it, is the way to the philosopher's stone and is another example of alchemy as ascent through descent. The rampant lion on the shield could be the Green Lion and the double-headed eagle on the left could be the animated mercury. So going from right to left, we have the raw ore of antimony, the Green Lion purified to become the regulus, the pure heart of the lion (that is pure antimony, called the star regulus of antimony) and then ending with the animated mercury, represented by the double-headed eagle. The anagram, V.I.T.R.I.O.L. reinforces the connection with the Green Lion through the original statement of Morienus' that "the Green lion is glass." Celestially speaking, Regulus, the brightest star in the constel-

illustrates how existing icons and images are appropriated to signify other meanings, perhaps parallel meanings.

lation of Leo, is the heart of the Lion. So if Regulus is the heart, stibnite, raw antimony ore is the lion itself.

Following this way of working with stibnite and antimony, Eirenaeus Philalethes[106] (1628–1665), in his *An Exposition upon Sir George Ripley's Preface* defines the Green Lion by what it *is not*:

> ***This hidden Body, or rather Chaos, the Philosophers have highly extolled and deeply concealed, but they usually call it their* Green Lyon, *which many mistaking apply to* Venus, *and some to* Vitriol, *which is all one in a manner,* Vitriol *being only Copper corroded by an embryonated Salt; but Fools, saith* Ripley *(in his Errors) call it the* Green Lyon.**[107]

And in *The Learned Sophies Feast,*[108] he defines the Green Lion by what it *is*:

> ***Whoso would lasting and eternal Fame***
> ***Deserve, Learn thou the Lyon Green to tame.***
> **...**
> ***This horrid Beast, which we our Lyon call,***
> ***Hath many other Names, that no man shall***
> ***The truth perceive, unless that God direct,***
> ***And on his darkened Mind a Light reflect.***
> **...**
> ***But it's because of the transcendent force***
> ***It hath, and for the rawness of its source,***
> ***Of which the like is no where to be seen,***
> ***That it of them is nam'd the Lyon Green.***
> **...**

106 The pseudonym of George Starkey, teacher of Sir Robert Boyle.

107 'An Exposition upon Sir George Ripley's Preface' in Eirenaeus Philalethes. *The Alchemical Works of Eirenaeus Philalethes*. S.M. Broddle ed. Boulder: Cinnabar Press, 1994) 169. Philalethes is expounding upon Sir George Ripley but the two alchemists are talking about two very different processes, the materials used overlap to some extent, but the two have very different approaches. Philalethes method uses the regulus of antimony and Ripley uses lead or antimony salt formed from the dissolution in concentrated wine vinegar. It appears that Philalethes, in "interpreting" Ripley, isn't so much elucidating Ripley's text, as he is working backwards, so to speak, in finding "scriptural" authority to back up his procedure and discoveries.

Be not deluded, for the truth is one,
'Tis not in many things, this is our Stone.
At first appearing in a Garb defil'd,
And to deal plainly, it is Saturn's Child.

So according to Philalethes, the Green Lion is Saturn's Child, as antimony was referred to due to its similarities to lead, that is, Saturn. So the Green Lion is stibnite, the sulphide ore of antimony, and not common vitriol.

> ***Learn then to know this* Green Lyon *and its preparation, which is all in all in the Art, it is the only knot, untie it, and you are as good as a Master; for whatever then remains is but to know the outward Regimen of Fire, for to help on Natures internal Work.***[109]

What Philalethes is talking about here is the formation of the Star Regulus of Antimony followed by a further amalgamation with silver. The Green Lion can be seen either as the Star regulus of antimony or as the raw stibnite. It is called the Green Lion "because of the transcendent force it hath, and for the rawness of its source." For the alchemists working in this manner, it is the prima materia of the Great Work. It is used as the means to purify and animate mercury. In *The Learned Sophies Feast,* Philalethes gives his process as

Their Lyon Green, they suffered him to prey
On Cadmus Sociates, and when the fray
Was over, they with Dian's Charms him ty'd
And made him under Waters to abide,
And wash'd him clean, and after gave him Wings
To fly, much like a Dragon, whose sharp Springs
Of fiery Water th' only way was found
To cause Apollo his Harp-strings to sound.
This is the true nymphs Bath, which we did try,
And prov'd to be the Wise Mens Mercury.[110]

Sir Robert Boyle "Of the Incalescence of Quicksilver with Gold, generously imparted by *B.R.*" *Philosophical Transactions, 10, 515-33 (no.122, 21 February 1676)*

108 Philalethes. 170 – 173.
109 Philalethes. 172, 173.
110 Philalethes. 172, 173.

This method given by Philalethes yields the animated mercury of a different type and through a different process, but both mercuries work on gold in a similar manner. That is, they dissolve gold as "warm water melts ice." This is the beginning of the Opus Magnum. Once the philosophical mercury has been obtained, the hardest part of the work is over, "for whatever then remains is but to know the outward Regimen of Fire." But without the Green Lion, there is no philosophical mercury. The Green Lion is where the work is initiated, where we may begin the journey through the labyrinth to the center.

They were amazed to see the last in the first and the very first in the last; in heaven they saw earthly things acting causally and in a heavenly manner, in the earth heavenly things in an earthly manner. *Proclus. On The Hieratic Art.*

In our search in the world of form and matter for this strange beast, remember that in the world-view of alchemy, a thing's physicality was only one aspect of that thing. The heart, for instance, was not only the physical pump in our chests but a living symbol of spirituality in a variety of aspects, all simultaneous with one another. The heart is, for the alchemist, the physical, mental and spiritual center of the person. So it is with the Green Lion. It is to be understood as an interdependent totality of its physical and spiritual or inner aspects, two pairs of a stereoscopic image.

This woodcut image of the Green Lion is one of the first depictions of the Green Lion. It is from the *Rosarium Philosophorum* 16th century.[111] There are two objects depicted here: the Lion, and the Sun, three if you include the blood but since the blood is a result of the Lion's action on the Sun I will consider it separately. The images of a Lion and the Sun are harmonious with each other and are even representative of each other as well as of a deeper symbolic meaning: that of a central ruler, the very core of life,

I am the true green and Golden Lion

In me all the secrets of the Philosophers are hidden

Ich bin der war grün vnnd guldisch Löwe ohn sorgen/
Inn mir steckt alle heimlichkeit der philosophen verborgen.

111 The first printing of this series was in the compendium *De alchemia opuscula complura veterum philosophorum.* Frankfurt. Cyriaeus Jacob 1550. The origins seem to be 1400 – 1450 Germany. Adam McLean. *The Silent Language: The Symbols of Hermetic Philosophy.* (Amsterdam: Pelikaan, 1994) 24.

being and existence. The Sun is the central fire of the heavens, expressed by the Lion, fire on earth. In the heavens, the astrological sign of Leo is ruled by the Sun. In our bodies, the heart is the central fire, our core, the very center of our selfhood. Where do we touch when we point to ourselves, but our hearts? "I," the king, the sun, the lion, the heart.

The color of the Lion is green, the Sun is of gold. Green is often associated with vegetative life, spirit, initiation, unripe, inexperienced, center color of the spectrum, and presence of the divine. In orthodox Christian iconography, green represents the indwelling of God in man, or its potential. Gold represents completion, perfection, unity, kingship, the sun, fully ripe. In this tradition, burnished gold when viewed from certain angles in certain light has the appearance of a radiant black. Gold used in this manner expresses or symbolizes visually what St. Dionysius the Areopagite (5th to 6th century) was trying to express in these words "...the brilliant darkness of a hidden silence."[112]

We could understand the Green Lion to mean an undeveloped Sun, while the Sun represents itself perfected. The action taking place in this image is the Lion biting into the Sun, eating the Sun, as the Sun bleeds. Blood is also a solar image, in that it relates to the heart. Blood is also represented by the alchemical principle of Sulphur or Soul. Putting this all together, the image could be read to mean, "unripe gold devours ripe gold releasing the soul of gold." In fact the motto associated with this image is "I am the green and Golden Lion, In me all the secrets of the Philosophers are hidden," reinforces the meaning that the Green Lion is unripe gold, the Golden Lion is pure ripe gold within which are the secrets of the philosophers symbolized by the blood, the soul. On one level, this interpretation suggests a direction of work, taking unripe gold to mean antimony.

112 The fuller quote from St. Dionysus' *Mystical Theology* is this, "where the mysteries of God's Word lie simple, absolute and unchangeable in the brilliant darkness of a hidden silence." From Dionysus Aeropagite. *Pseudo-Dionysus: The Complete Works*. (NY: Paulist Press, 1987) 135.

This image can also be seen as directing one through a stage on the path towards gnosis, that is, the knowledge of and union with the divine. And as gnosis involves ourselves, we turn to ourselves. We turn to our hearts. We reach out to the divine by turning inward towards our heart. It is the heart that is the physical point of contact between the human and the divine.

Heart, gold, sun, lion – let each of these words be interchangeable with each other, along with the words; green, immature, center, initiate, hesychia/silence, water of life, near to the divine. Let each meaning have equal sway.

Contemplation of the image will reveal more about the Green Lion, not in the sense of codes, but rather as a living symbol – in which the meanings shift, flow and circulate. True symbols illuminate and reveal, rather than obscure their unspoken center. As we turn over in our mind and meditate on the qualities, first singly and then in relation to the other terms, allowing the various meanings to arise and fall away – not fixing or crystallizing anything yet, but letting the form take shape in the twilight and in the periphery – there is our Green Lion.

مَا وَسِعَنِي سَمَائِي
وَلا أَرْضِي،
وَلَكِنِّي وَسِعَنِي
قَلْبُ عَبْدِي
الْمُؤْمِن

My earth does not encompass Me, nor does My heaven, but the heart of My servant, the man of true faith, does encompass Me. *Hadith cited by Ibn 'Arabī. Futūḥāt. Chapter 367.*

The immature-self penetrates the shell of the central-self, opening to the divine. The initiate penetrates the shell of the heart and releases the waters of life.

We can begin to see, as through a glass darkly, the dimensions of this symbol. Symbols are windows between worlds, and like a window it has a frame, a context which should not, cannot be ignored. With each text, with each image, with each circumstance, it must be questioned anew.

To give some context to this, I will return to Morienus' and Khālid's conversation recorded in *Liber de Compositione alchimiae.*

It concerns the instruction given by Morienus Romanus, who, as was already noted, a Christian monk. And it is from Morienus that we hear the words "Green Lion" spoken. Who was Morienus? According to legend he was taught by Stephanos of Alexandria (ca. 7th century), who had explicated the alchemy that was transmitted by Zosimos of Panopolis.

This is the alchemy practiced.

Gnosticism, and particularly Christianity, which sees itself as the true gnosis,[113] is one of the contexts of this conversation. Stephanos of Alexandria, while knowing the practical, is mystical in nature, more concerned with the transmutation of the soul of humanity into "gold" than the base metals. As Stephanos wrote, "what's the best of the species of Chrysokolla compared to Beauty."

As noted above, Morienus was considered to be a student of Stephanos. Now whether this is to be taken literally or as a metaphor, the fact is, the alchemy that Stephanos describes, and the teaching methods of example and enigmas is the same alchemy and method that Morienus demonstrates to Khālid.

As shown earlier, for Stephanos there were two "chemistries" – one *mythic*, a multiplicity of words, lost in the noise. The other, *mystic chemistry*, that deals with the universe through deliberation on the creation and its method "consists of celestial images and whatever is necessary is accomplished by method."

Khālid ibn Yazīd represents another context, that of Islam and its gnostic and scientific traditions. According to the bibliographer An-Nadīm (970 CE), Khālid ibn Yazīd supported the arts and was "the first Moslem to have medical, astronomical and chemical writings translated for him."[114] In fact, this was the beginning of the translation of Greek scientific and philo-

113 See St Paul's letter to Timothy warning him of the "contradictions of so-called gnosis." (1Timothy 6:20).

114 Fück, J.W. "The Arabic Literature on Alchemy According to An-Nadīm." Ambix Vol. IV. Nos. 3&4. (Feb 1951) 121. Khālid ibn Yazīd ibn Mu'āwiya (c.668–704 or 708) was a son of the second Umayyad calif Yazīd I.

sophical works into Arabic. Further evidence of this early translation work is found in an Arabic translation of Zosimos dated 659 CE, 27 years after the death of the Prophet Muhammad.[115]

O marvel! a garden amidst fires!
My heart has become capable of every form:
It is a pasture for gazelles
And a convent for Christian monks,
And a temple for idols and the pilgrims Ka'ba
And the tables of the Tora and the book of the Koran.
I follow the religion of Love:
Whatever way Love's camels take,
That is my religion and my faith.
Muhyiddīn ibn al-'Arabī. Tarjumān al-Ashwāq.

Sufism, an Islamic mystical tradition, is also gnostic in that it describes paths and techniques for the ascent of the soul to God, or perhaps more accurately, *fanā*, annihilation in God or nullification of self in the divine presence.[116] "Like the flame of the Candle in the presence of the sun, he is non-existent, though existent in formal calculation," is how the poet Rūmī describes *fanā.*

F*anā* has three stages. The first is when the attributes of the initiate are annihilated and they take on the attributes of God. The second is annihilation in vision, where the soul is immersed in the primordial uncreated light of God. The third and final stage is that one's vision of annihilation is annihilated. The initiate is immersed in the existence of God. "To discover the clarity of this black light is to find the green water of life."[117] Spiritual ascent in Christianity as well has three stages – *via purgativa*, purification; *via illuminativa*, illumination with love and gnosis; *unio mystica*, mystical union with God, where the spirit sees beyond all vision.

The start of this journey is the initiation which is conferred upon the novice by the *pir*, the teacher, the *starets*, the spiritual friend who guides the novice on their way.

Morienus said to him: 'O king, may God enrich you... You have approached me as an equal in spirit, and now I see by your affection, excellence, and discrimination that one such as I should have no reason to keep from you anything of that which you seek, for you are indeed a man of good intentions

115 Stapelton, H. E. "An Alchemical Compilation of the Thirteenth Century." *Memoirs of the Asiatic Society of Bengal*, 3, 1910. 67.

116 Dying to self through transmutation. See discussion in Annemarie Schimmel. *Mystical Dimensions of Islam.* (University of North Carolina Press, 1975).

117 Schimmel. 144.

as well as deeds and most virtuous. Very well, you have attained to your initiation and instruction simply and with the greatest of ease. May the Creator be praised!'[118]

The structure of *Liber de Compositione alchimiae* has a similar form to Sufi tales of encounters between Christian monks and Sufis. The dialogue can be seen as an experienced adept from one tradition (Orthodox Christianity) teaching what he has realized to an aspiring novice from another tradition (Islam) using the language of alchemy to teach and guide the aspirant. An example of this is from ibn Sīna, in his recounting of his master in alchemy Jacob the Jew. Ibn Sīna, quoting Jacob, writes,

Jacob the Jew, a man of penetrating mind, also taught me many things, and I shall repeat to you what he taught me: if you want to be a philosopher of nature, to whichever religion you belong, listen to the instructed man of whatever religion, because the law of the philosopher says: thou shalt not kill, thou shalt not steal, thou shalt not commit adultery, do unto others as you do to yourself, and don't utter blasphemies.[119]

Perhaps it is in the dialogue, spoken in the language of the birds, that alchemy resides. In the twilight language of dreams, let us consider the Green Lion in this context by taking a closer look at what these terms that describe or make up the symbol of the Green Lion represent or strive to convey within Christianity and Islam.

Be still and know that I am God.
Psalm 46:10

The Sun and Lion in both traditions are associated with kingship, royalty and gold. In short, it is the astrological sense of the Sun and Lion that is shared by both traditions, as is the association of the heart with both the Sun and the Lion. We can see how "lion" resonates with "heart," in words

118 Morienus. 1974. 9.

119 Patai. *The Jewish Alchemists*. 97.

like "courage." In a material expression of the same lion, heart relationship, we have stibnite and regulus of antimony. The Green Lion is stibnite, Heart of the Green Lion is the regulus, pure and stellated, bright as the heart of Leo, from which the waters of life pour forth. It is interesting to note here that water spouts in the form of lions heads are found on fountains throughout what was once the Roman Empire. They were originally used in Egypt, where the flooding of the Nile occurred when the sun was entering Leo. Celestially speaking, the Lion is devouring the Sun releasing the water of life. The Egyptian irrigation gates had lion heads carved in them from which the life giving water of the Nile came forth and ever since we have used waterspouts carved as lions heads to grace our fountains, greening our gardens.

The color green in Islam has great significance. It signifies, amongst other things, tranquility, closeness to the divine, and *Khidr* (the Verdant One, the Green One) who was the companion of the Prophet Mohammed, the patron saint of travelers, the immortal who drank from the waters of life. He would meet mystics and invest them with the robe of initiation the *khirqa*. Green is associated with the *pir*, the spiritual friend, teacher, who would initiate and guide the *murid*, the novice, disciple. Attar (1200 CE) wrote, "The Pir is the red sulphur, and his breast the green ocean." We have here an allusion to alchemical transmutation: the red sulphur, *kibrīt aḥmar*, also in Morienus' list of things needed for the Great Work. Red sulphur was also called *qalb al-asad*, "heart of the lion."[120] Once again we come to the heart, *qalb* in Arabic, its root meaning is actually transformation and change.[121] The heart is the place where the attention is focused in some forms of *dhikr* – *dhikr al-qalb*, with the heart, and *dhikr as-sirr*, with the innermost heart. *Dhikr* is a repetition of a phrase vocalized or recited mentally, remembering God. It is this practice that softens the heart from stone to flesh.

لا إله إلا الله

La ilaha ilallah

There is no god but Allah

I saw my Lord with the Eye of my Heart and I said to Him 'Who art Thou' and He said 'Thou'. *Manṣūr al-Ḥallāj.*

Го́споди, Иису́се Христе́, поми́луй меня́.

Lord Jesus Christ, have mercy on me.

Κύριε Ἰησοῦ Χριστέ, ἐλέησόν με

120 Alfred Siggel. *Decknamen in Der Arabischen Alchemistischen Literatur.* (Berlin: Akademie-Verlag, 1951) 47.

121 In Arabic essentially only the consonants are written, so *qalb*, when written, appears as *qlb*. Any other words written with the root *qlb* are related. Other meanings also resonate as is shown in *'ilm al-hurūf*, the science of letters, a technique for analyzing and

A similar approach to the heart is taken in the teachings of the Desert Fathers on the Prayer of the Heart, "Lord Jesus Christ, Son of God, have mercy on me." This too is done with the attention on the heart, as well as vocally or mentally. The heart is visualized with the recitation. *Hesychia*, silence, is the state one is trying to achieve with the practice – This dynamic silence is symbolized by the color green. Green, as noted above, also signifies the indwelling of God. As St. Gregory Palamas writes about the *hesychasts*, the practioners of *hesychia*, quoting St. John from his *Ladder of Divine Ascent*, "The *hesychast* is one who seeks to circumscribe the incorporeal in his body."[122]

Within the heart is an unfathomable depth. *St. Macarius of Egypt.*

I have looked into my own heart; it is there that I have seen Him; He was nowhere else. *Rūmī*

God has sent the Spirit of His Son into our hearts, crying Abba! Father! *Galatians 4:6*

The heart is the innermost body within the body... the shrine of the intelligence and the chief intellectual organ of the body. *St. Gregory Palamas.*

When asked by Khālid what is the matter to be worked on, Morienus replied,

> ***Truly this matter is created by God which is firmly captive within you yourself, inseparable from you, wherever you be. This thing is extracted from you, for you are its mine.***[123]

How are we to understand this "thing?" To what does it refer? Is it a physical thing from the body? Possibly blood or perhaps even urine. As we have seen urine plays an important role in alchemy. Or does it mean, as St. Luke writes, "The Kingdom of God is within you."[124]

Or is it the ability and will to create something where once was nothing? Is this the image in which we were created? So here we are at the entry point of the work, at the mouth of the labyrinth.

Find a quiet place to sit alone and in silence, bow your head and shut your eyes. Breathe softly; look with your mind into your heart; recollect your mind – that is, all its thoughts – and bring them down from your mind into your heart. As you breathe, repeat: "Lord Jesus Christ, have mercy on me," whether quietly with your lips, or only in your mind. Make an effort to banish all thoughts; be calm and patient, and repeat this exercise frequently. *Philokalia Saint Symeon the New Theologian. The Way of the Pilgrim. Anonymous. p8.*

So, what is the Green Lion?

meditating on the layers of meanings a word and text may have. For instance, words with the same letters but with a different order share a meaning. So that *qalb, qlb* is related to *qbl, qābil* meaning receptivity. It is also related to the word *qiblah* or point of orientation, pointing to the *Ka'bah*, the House of God, that is, spiritually speaking, the heart.

122 St. Gregory Palamas. *Gregory Palamas. The Triads.* (NJ: Paulist Press, 1983) 45.

123 Morienus. 1974. 26, 27.

124 Luke 17:21

It is prayer, it is remembrance, creative stillness, creative silence. It is a water that opens our heart. It is our attitude of openness. It is that which opens the heart. Unripe Sol devours ripe Sol, releasing the Sulphur of Sol. It is antimony ore, it is green vitriol, it is aqua regia. The Green Lion can really only be said to represent one thing only when all the terms in the phrase have also been defined, even if only loosely so. With each correct revision within a chosen framework, the terms come into sharper focus – we approach mastership as to what and how to proceed in the work. The Green Lion is the thing which reduces Sol to its parts and abstracts its Sulphur, its Blood. As the jackal changes dead flesh into its own living flesh, so the Blood of Sol is absorbed into the Blood of the Green Lion. When contemplating the Green Lion, hold the various meanings in mind along with the "thing" it comprises. And when you are satisfied that you have the Green Lion, proceed with the work.

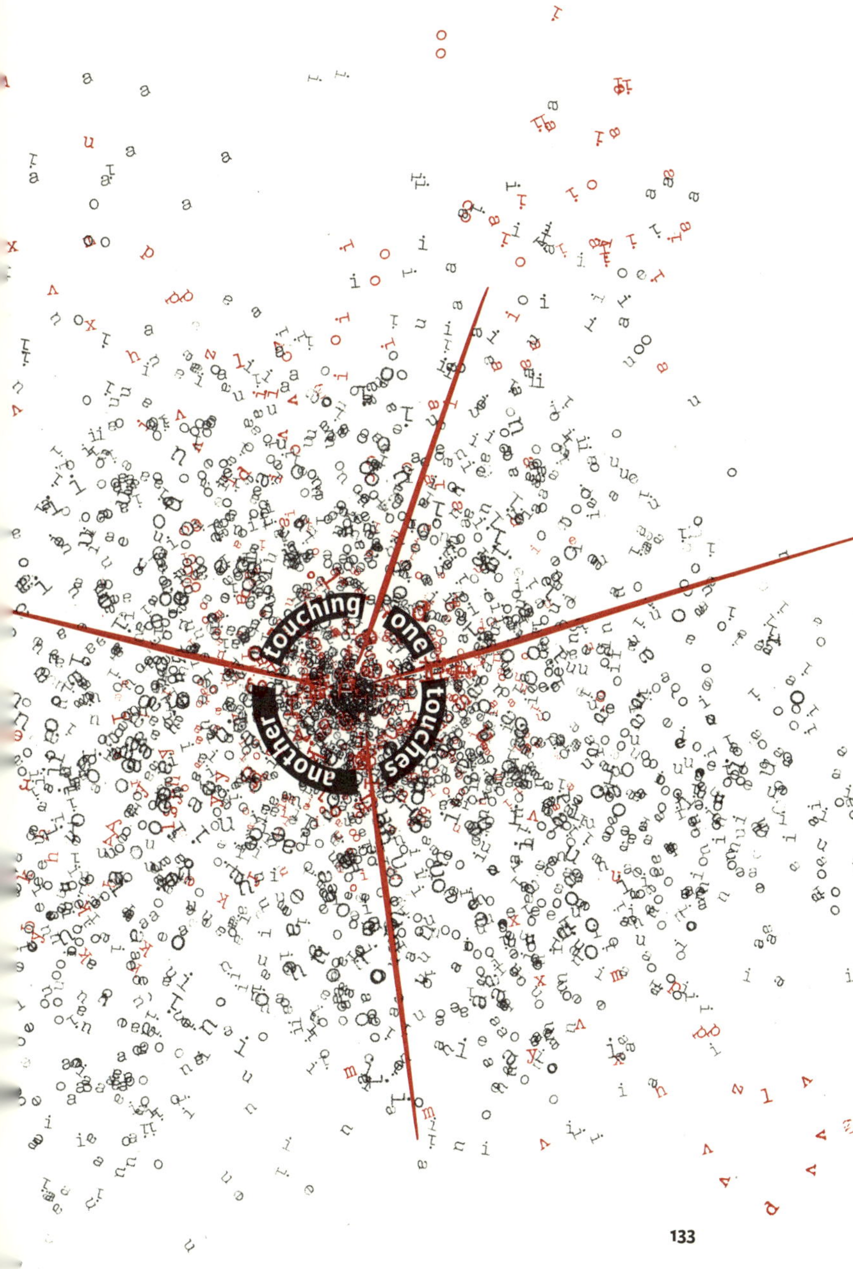
touching one touches another

This could happen also in this way,

If you first of all separated the body from man

(and obviously from

yourself)

and then the soul which forms it

and, very thouroughly

sense-perception

and desires and passions

and all the rest of such fooleries,

since

they incline very much to mortal.

Plotinus. Ennead V.3.9.

In this silence we descend deeper, and approach the heart of the gnostic. This is the multi-dimensional center of an existent being, the isthmus, the thin boundary that is the symbolic realm between the two realities of existence and non-existence, and is the place of contact, of unity, of these two realities.

First of all, we must bear in mind that the universe is a single living being. *Iamblichus. On The Mysteries. (IV.12.195)*

In the hermetic view of the cosmos, unity extends throughout – all is one. All is interconnected. Hippocrates observed that when one part of the body suffers, another part might be affected as well.[125] He called this phenomenon *sympatheia* meaning "same feeling." The Greek philosophers following Hippocrates expanded the concept to the created world. It indicates the continuum throughout all aspects of the cosmos: space, matter, and the propagation and sequence of phenomena. Synesius (ca 400), in his *On Dreams,* states "...all the parts of this grand whole, animated with a common life, should be united by an intimate relation, as members of the same body."[126]

The theurgic art in many cases links together stones, plants, animals, aromatic substances, and other such things that are sacred, perfect and god like, and then from all these composes an integrated and pure receptacle. *On the Mysteries. Iamblicus. Book V.23.233. p269*

The renaissance philosopher Marsilio Ficino (1433–1499) amplifies: "the parts of the world, like parts of a single animal, all deriving from a single author, are joined to each other by the communion of a single nature."[127] Posidonius (2nd–1st century BCE), observing the influence of the Moon on the tides explained this action by tension in the *pneuma*, noting that there is a *sympathy* between Moon and water observed in the rising and falling of the tides. The parts are held together and interconnected by *pneuma*, a subtle mix of the finest purest Fire and the finest purest Air.[128] Pneuma permeates the entire world as its soul, as its essence and is the means by which objects can

Transplant mallows in your garden, but eat them not. *Symbol 38 Pythagorean Symbols*

125 Hippocrates. *De alimento* XXIII. "Conflux one, conspiration one, all things in sympathy; all the parts as forming a whole, and severally the parts in each part, with reference to the work." *Hippocrates Collected Works I.* Hippocrates. W. H. S. Jones. (Cambridge: Harvard UP. 1984) 351.

126 Synesius. *On Dreams by Saint Synesios*. Trans. Isaac Myer. (Philadelphia: Myer. 1888) 4.

127 Marsilio Ficino. *Commentary on Plato's Symposium On Love.* Trans. Sears Jayne. (Dallas: Spring Publications, 1985) 127.

128 For Synesius these are particles of fine air and fire or "the flower of matter" as he quotes from the Sibylline Verses. Synesios. *On Dreams by Saint Synesios*, 16.

interact with each other at a distance such as the Moon, Sun, and sea. Ficino demonstrates this idea with further examples:

> ***Thus the lodestone draws iron, and amber draws chaff, and sulphur, fire; the Sun turns many flowers and leaves towards itself, and the Moon, the waters; Mars is accustomed to stir the winds, and the various plants also attract to themselves various kinds of animals.***[129]

Musical resonance as well demonstrates this link between like things. For instance, the "E" string plucked on one guitar will cause the "E" string on a guitar across the room to vibrate. Today, of course, we explain these things differently.

The four elements are the elements both of the heavens and of generation. Hence the heavens are of a fifth essence, besides the four elements; but are mingled from the simple elements. *Procl Comm. Parmen.p311*

For alchemy, *sympatheia* is an important concept and is crucial in understanding some alchemical practices, in that the pneuma is expressed as the *quintessence*. The quintessence – the fifth essence or fifth element, although related by name, stands in opposition to Aristotle's fifth element of space – the ether. In Aristotle's cosmology, the two realms, the heavenly and the sublunary are distinctly separate.[130] Aristotle's fifth element is "pure and divine" and apart from the material world of the four elements of Fire, Air, Water, and Earth. Alchemically speaking, the quintessence is something that shares in and permeates both realms. At first it is by analogy.

The all permeates everything and surrounds everything. *Corpus Hermeticm. XII.23.*

> ***...philosophers called heaven the quintessence with respect to the four elements, because heaven is in itself incorruptible and immutable, and not the recipient of stray impressions, unless it be made by the will of God. In this way, this thing which we seek (the quintessence) is the same with respect to the four qualities of our body...***[131]

129 Marsilio Ficino. *Commentary on Plato's Symposium On Love.* Trans. Sears Jayne. (Dallas: Spring Publications, 1985) 127.

130 Aristotle. *On The Heavens.* Trans. W.K.C. Gutherie. (Cambridge: Harvard UP. 1953) 17.

131 John of Rupescissa. *De Consideratione Quintae Essentie rerum omnium, opus.* (Basile, 1561) 19–20.

Here, John of Rupescissa (1300–1365) is suggesting that there is a lower quintessence – the purest substance of corruptible things, just as there is a higher quintessence, the "heaven of our Lord God." He also suggests that the lower quintessence permeates the created world as the heavenly quintessence permeates the heavens and all space. About a hundred years later in *De vita libri tres* (1489), Marsilio Ficino states that the two quintessences are "practically the same thing."

> ***The world generates everything through it (since, indeed, all things generate through their own spirit); and we can call it both 'the heavens' and 'quintessence.' It is practically the same thing in the world's body as in our body...***[132]

Keep this in mind: the meaning of quintessence shifts between the material and non-material throughout alchemy, and sometimes the word slides in meaning to imply both simultaneously. It strains to point to something beyond language, strains to explain a non-dual reality through dualistic language, strains to explain how the finite can be the matrix for the infinite.

A root text of quintessence theory in alchemy is *De Consideratione Quintae Essentie* (DQE) by John of Rupescissa.[133] In this work Rupescissa not only posits a material substance for the pneuma, the quintessence, but he also puts it into the context of a larger alchemical theory, in fact, a larger cosmological theory. That is, the role of the quintessence functions as an intermediary in the relationship between the fully divine and fully material. It shares in and permeates[134] both the divine and the material, establishing a harmonic and dynamic balance throughout the cosmos.

132 Marsilio Ficino. *Three Books on Life (De vita libri tres)*. Trans. Carol Kaske and John Clark. (New York: Medieval & Renaissance Texts, 1998) 257.

133 For a study of John of Rupescissa and his work see Leah DeVun. *Prophecy, Alchemy, and the End of the World*. (New York: Columbia UP, 2009).

134 Here is another parallel with the *Emerald Tablet* that states, "It penetrates all dense things."

In particular, the quintessence preserves the body by adding any quality to bring about a balance of the elements, manifested as humors, within the body. This is the definition of an elixir. An elixir in general, as mentioned earlier, is a composition that will bring the matter in question to its perfection. It does this by bringing balance to the body, augmenting harmoniously the qualities or elements involved in the composition of the matter. According to this theory each thing would have its own elixir, its own particular composition that would bring it to perfection.

> ***The fifth element has thus been made incorruptible in itself. It isn't dry and hot as with fire, nor wet and cold, like water, nor too hot and wet like air, and it isn't dry and cold as with earth. But instead it is the fifth element, strong against the opposites, incorruptible as heaven: that, when it is necessary, pours in the wet quality of the part, and sometimes hot, sometimes cold, sometimes dry. So the fifth element is the root of life, which the most High has created in nature.***[135]

It is the presence of the quintessence in the corruptible sublunary realm that allows the possibility for the perfection of the body through the balance of the elements of which it is comprised. The quintessence permeates all but in some things it is more accessible and potent. And, one of the most potent sources is wine. Speaking about the quintessence of wine, Rupescissa relates an experiment that demonstrates its power of preservation.

> ***If any bird or piece of flesh or fish is immersed in it, it will not be corrupted while it remains in it. Therefore, how much more will it preserve the animated and living flesh of our body from all corruption?***[136]

For him the quintessence of wine is a channel or medium for the force or virtue that supports and preserves life that it

135 Rupescissa. *De Consideratione Quintae Essentie (DQE)*. 19–20.

136 Rupescissa. *DQE*. 21.

shares with the One. It will become clear however that what he is talking about, materially, is ethanol distilled from wine and concentrated and purified through further distillations.

But yet it is more.

To begin, wine, in its full being, arises at the intersection of myth and matter, a result of the fermentation of grapes; its affects on humans; and all that the vine and its results symbolize. It is the source for a most potent quintessence, materially and symbolically.

One story from the *Dionysiaca* of Nonnos, tells of the discovery of wine. One day that wild twice-born[137] son of Zeus, Dionysus, saw a snake sucking the grape, fermented juice trickling down its throat.[138] Seeing this and remembering a certain oracle of Rhea, Dionysus then dug into the rock and hollowed a pit with the sharp prongs of his earth burrowing pick, making it like a wine press. He took his thyrsus and made it like a sickle and reaped the grapes. With the harvest of ripe grapes laid in the hole, he stomped on the grapes, releasing the intoxicating liquor.

This story touches on some of the distinguishing features of Dionysus – cutting, tearing apart, and wine where resides that wild untamed spirit of the vine.

Dionysus's followers would, in ecstatic frenzy, tear apart living animals. Euripides depicts this murderous frenzy in the *Bacchae,* in particular when, after Pentheus bans the worship of Dionysus and refuses to recognize the god, the Maenads tear Pentheus apart,

Hymn to Dionysus

To Dionysos
incense - storax

I call upon loud-roaring,
reveling Dionysos,

primeval, two-natured,
thrice-born Bacchic lord,

savage, ineffable, secretive,
two-horned and two-shaped,

ivy-covered, bull faced,
warlike, howling, pure.

You take raw flesh in triennial feasts,

wrapped in foliage, decked
with grape clusters,

resourceful Eubouleus,
immortal god sired by Zeus

when he mated with
Persphone in unspeakable
union.

Hearken to my voice, O
blessed one,

you and your fair-girdled
nurses,

breathe on me in a spirit of
perfect kindness.

The Orphic Hymns. Translated Athanassakis & Wolkow. 2013.

137 Proclus recounts in his *Hymn to Minerva* a story about the origins of Dionysus where after he is killed and dismembered by the Titans, his heart is put aside as they prepare to eat the body. Minerva brought the heart to Zeus who prepared a potion from the heart and gave it to Semele to drink. Semele gives birth to Dionysus and so born a second time. *Hymn to Minerva* in Thomas Taylor. *The Eleusinian and Bacchic Mysteries*, (New York: De Vinne Press, 1891) 225–26.

138 Nonnos. *Dionysiaca. Vol. 1.* Trans. W.H.D. Rouse. (Cambridge: Harvard UP, 1984) 420–421.

limb-by-limb. This kind of frenzied, ecstatic tearing apart is called in Greek, *sparagmos*. There is another side of the powers of Dionysus, in his boyhood,

> ***He rent rams, skins and all, and clove them piecemeal and cast the dead bodies on the ground; and again with his hands he neatly put their limbs together, and immediately they were alive and browsed on the green pasture.***[139]

But it begins with *sparagmos*. This is the true heart of wine, and the first step in its making. Cut from the vine, stomped and crushed, the juice pressed from the crushed grapes, after a primary fermentation, was sealed into jars and partially or fully buried. The following spring the jars were opened revealing the juice transformed into wine full of the spirit of fire.

Plutarch records the date; "At Athens people consecrate the fresh wine on the eleventh day of the month Anthesterion, calling the day Pithogia." Pithogia fell as early as February to as late as March – essentially an early spring festival. It was a period of celebration when the large clay jars *pithoi* were opened and the wine was drunk. It covered three festivals: a children's festival, a festival of the dead where the spirits of the dead came from the underworld, and a sacred marriage to Dionysus. In these festivals we see here a focus on respectively: newness, spirits on earth, and a union of earthy and divine.

In the iconography of Jesus Christ, another deity twice-born through his resurrection, we encounter a more mystic expression of the *sparagmos* of wine-making, one of the most potent Christian symbols, that of the "Mystic Winepress." It is an allegory of the spilling of Christ's blood on the cross as grapes are pressed into wine.

To understand this, let us look more closely at the result of this process and examine the physical phenomena of wine itself. We see that it can be divided mechanically through filtering,

139 Oppian. *Cynegetica*. Trans. A.W. Mair. (Cambridge: Harvard UP, 1963) 185.

settling, and decanting. These processes yield the wine itself: tartar crystals of potassium bitartrate that form during fermentation; and the lees, the residual solids that settle out, dead yeast, grape skins etc. Wine divided by simple distillation, yields spirit, phlegm, and feces.[140] Of course with more careful distillations and separations of the spirit, phlegm, and feces, more products can be isolated. In fact, this process is the beginning of the end of the Three Principles and Four Elements theories. Once the dividing begins, it is only a question of the tools and resolution of description that will determine where it ends. A more systematic and complete analysis of wine yields water, ethanol, methanol, other alcohols, acids, volatile acids, sugars, pigments, phenols, minerals, vitamins, terpenes, and glycerol. In fact, thousands of compounds can be identified.

In *De Consideratione Quintae Essentie* Rupescissa focuses on the spirit of wine, or *aqua ardens*. Wine, by simple distillation, produces aqua ardens, "burning water," also called aqua vitae, "water of life." The first distillation yields about 30% - 50% alcohol, water and other volatiles. In choosing a wine to work with, remember that while the quality of the wine is not crucial, it is nevertheless important that you...

> ***Do not take wine that is too watery, nor black wine, earthy, tasteless, but wine that is noble, fertile, flavorful and fragrant, the best you can find. And distill it canonically many times, until you make the best aqua ardens you know how to do. Distill it three to***

140 Spirit – hot, subtle, pure, clear cordial, and balsamical. It is a very small portion of the wine and is the source of the quintessence. Phlegm – what remains after the spirit is distilled. It is putrid, insipid, cold, and narcotic. Feces – what remains when the phlegm is distilled. It is a viscous, corrosive matter.

seven times: and this is the aqua ardens, to which modern doctors have not attained. This water is the matter from which is extracted the quintessence.[141]

Canonical distillation,[142] done with a gentle heat, usually provided by horse dung, is not a fast distillation, but a slow drop-by-drop process. Tradition holds that the time between drops should equal the time it takes to say a pater noster. Rupescissa shows a few ways of working with the environment you are in and the tools you have to provide a gentle heat for the work with the quintessence. The vessels and heat are arranged in this way. One should take:

...the best horse manure,[143] ***and pack it in what ever vessel, or make a pit in the ground, line it all with ashes and in the middle well packed manure. Arrange a circulation distillation vessel up to the middle or more. What is necessary is that the whole head of the vessel remains in place in the cold air, so that which has ascended by the heat of manure, there again is converted into water by the power of cold air...***[144]

This is a very slow distillation, as decomposing horse dung produces a heat of about 40°C, while alcohol boils at 78.5°C. Another slow distillation is to, in the summer, take the aqua ardens and set the vessel "to reverberate by the strong sun, and day and night without your effort, leave to rest."[145] The point is that a steady heat at around 40°C will do, whether from a pile of dung, the Sun, a heating mantle, or a radiator in a four flight walk up.

141 Rupescissa. *DQE.* 29–30.

142 In an Italian translation of an unidentified manuscript of *De quintessence*, the same paragraph expands and defines it canonically. "Then distil it... do that not by means of a rapid distillation, but drop by drop, so that it is distilled three, seven, ten times." Author's translation. *Trattato sulla Quintessenza* (Rome: Mediterranee, 1998) 22–23.

143 The Latin term *ventri equi* literally means "horses belly" or "horses womb." It is, however, the phrase used to describe the temperature achieved through decaying horse manure which is about 40°C. *Palestra-Pharmaceutica Chymica-Galenica.* Felix Palacios. (Madrid: Ibara, 1768) 168–69.

144 Rupescissa. *DQE.* 35–36.

145 Rupescissa. *DQE.* 36.

So with a gentle heat, the wine is slowly distilled, and the first aqua ardens comes over. This is approximately 30% alcohol; the rest is water and other volatiles. This distillate is the first aqua ardens, which is then distilled, leaving more of the water and impurities behind, increasing the concentration of alcohol in the aqua ardens. This second aqua ardens is then itself distilled. This process is repeated, "at least three to seven times and continually digested in a horse's womb."[146]

Pater noster qui es in coelis sanctificetur nomen tuum. Adveniat regnum tuum. Fiat voluntas tua sicut in coela et in terra. Panem nostrum quotidianum da nobis hodie. Et dimitte nobis debita nostra, sicut et nos demittimus debitoribus nostris. Et ne nos inducas in temptationem. Sed libera nos a malo. Amen.

This then, is the final aqua ardens as purified of the elements as possible. This is a concentrated aqua ardens, also called spirits of wine, alcohol, or ethanol, and it can be up to 95% pure. Higher concentrations aren't practical, as pure ethanol is hydroscopic and will absorb water from the atmosphere. This concentrated aqua ardens is not yet the quintessence but very nearly so. For the quintessence to arise, the final stage of circulation is necessary. Circulation is key to making the quintessence. It not only further separates the quintessence from the corruptible elements but it opens it to the virtues of the heavens. Through circulation, the spirit of wine becomes the quintessence that contains all the virtues of the heavens.

In the processes outlined below, note the allusions to the *Emerald Tablet* in the images of ascent and descent of the spirit (see page 55 for full text). In Alexandrian alchemy, this ascent, this circulation of the spirit rising from the matrix and then descending was seen to verify, or to be verified by, the *Emerald Tablet*, whose central image is one of circulation, of ascent and descent.

The instrument used is a "pelican." It is the appearance of this apparatus that evokes the image of the pelican. It was believed that pelicans would cut their breasts with their beaks, allowing their blood to flow, feeding their young. This

O Zosimos... explain to me the operation of this secret... 'The inferior with the high-ranking, and the high-ranking with the inferior.' *Zosimos. Muṣhaf as-Ṣuwar. The Book of Pictures.*

146 Rupescissa. *DQE*. 41. See page 144 n143.

image in Christian iconography expresses selfless giving, compassion, and the redemptive power of the blood of Jesus.

There will distill forth a Spirit of such a fragrant smell that the fragrancy of all flowers, and compounded perfumes are not to be compared to it. *John French. The Art of Distillation. 73-74*

The instrument takes many forms but the most common has two spherical chambers, upper and lower. The upper is slightly smaller than the lower and there is an opening between them and an opening in top of the upper chamber. There are two to eight tubes running from the side of the upper chamber to the sides of the lower chamber. The tubes allow the condensate to flow back into the lower chamber. The lower chamber of the vessel is filled no more than half with the final aqua ardens (95% spirits of wine). The vessel is sealed and placed in the prepared manure so that the lower chamber is covered and the head is in the cold air. The colder the air, the more dynamic is the circulation.

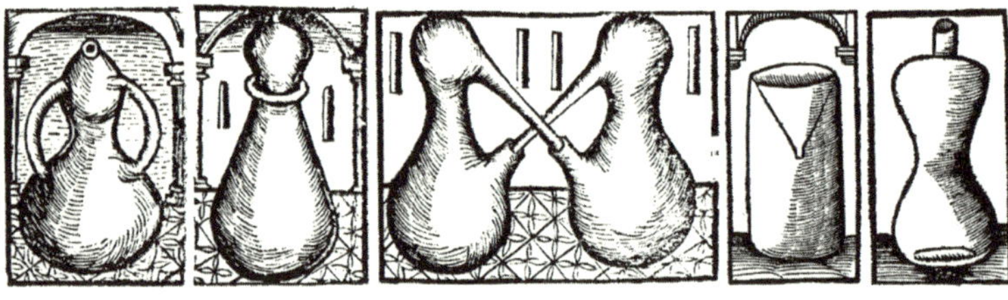

A friend has described this odour as resembling the dewy earth on a June morning with the hint of growing flowers in the air, the breath of the wind over heather and hill, and the sweet smell of the rain on the parched earth. *Archibald Cockren. Alchemy Rediscovered and Restored. 123.*

Thus in the abysmal dark The soul is known by scent. *Heraclitus Fragment 38*

You can see that it is so wonderfully shaped instrument so that by the power of fire it ascended and drips into the vessel through the channels of the arms, is brought back again, and again to ascend and again descend continually day and night, until the aqua ardens is converted into the quintessence by the will of God from heaven.[147]

And not just once but,

... up to a thousand times, and by continuous ascent and descent it is raised up to such a height, it becomes glorified. It may be a composition almost incorruptible as heaven, and of the nature of heaven. Therefore it is called the quintessence.[148]

147 Rupescissa. *DQE.* 30–31.

148 Rupescissa. *DQE.* 31.

After this continuous circulation and the flask is opened, a scent will fill the air that is[149]

> ***the most marvelous such that no worldly fragrance can equal. It seems to have descended from on high of the most glorious God. So that if the vessel were lying in the corner of the house because of the fragrance of the quintessence (what a wondrous and sum of miracles it is) by an invisible chain would attract to itself all who enter in.***[150]

When this happy event takes place, the whole house will be filled with a most wonderfully sweet fragrance; then will be the day of the Nativity of the most blessed Preparation. *The Testament of Cremer. The Hermetic Museum, Vol 2: 75-76*

This is the quintessence.

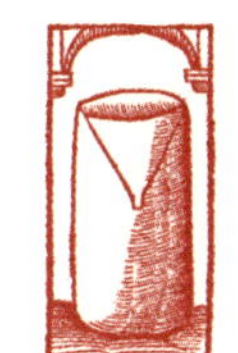

The thing to emphasize here is circulation. It is the most crucial stage of the process.

Once I was experimenting with various circulation set-ups, using, like Rupescissa, readily available materials. One glass circulation device allowed a very clear view of the process. As the quintessence was heated, it reached the necessary vapor saturation for condensation to occur. What I observed were very small clouds forming at the top near the cooling surface. Considering their source as they formed, the words from the *Emerald Tablet* I was translating at the time came to mind, "the higher comes from the lower." And soon tiny droplets of the quintessence began to gently rain down from above into the solution below from which it came. And again, the words from the *Emerald Tablet* resonated, "the lower comes from the higher." Here we see how the practice illuminates and verifies the text. And as the *Emerald Tablet* further states, it takes on the power of the high and low. Through this circulation, the quintessence rises and falls, carrying with it the powers and virtues of the higher and the lower. It is able to penetrate all dense things. And through this penetration, the quintessence is able to extract the quintessence from other things.

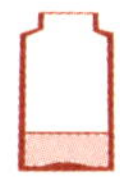

> ***God of heaven conferred such virtue to the quintessence that it extracts from all fruit, branch, root,***

149 The very pleasant scent of the quintessence is a theme that runs throughout alchemy and is in fact a major clue in uncovering some meanings.

150 Rupescissa. *DQE.* 32–33.

flower, herb, meat, seed and any species of things and from any medicinal thing, all the virtues and properties and natures and effects, [...]
And it will be a hundred times better because of the quintessence than it would be without it.[151]

According to Rupescissa, simply soaking any of the aforementioned items in the quintessence for three hours extracts their virtues, properties, natures and effects. This solution is filtered, then distilled and circulated.

Rupescissa also brings Hermetic aspects into the practice as well, such as the idea that the quintessence is "our heaven" on Earth. As Heaven is strengthened by the character and nature of the stars such as the Sun, so is the Earthly quintessence inflected by the addition of "terrestrial stars" such as gold.

حَقّاً يَقِيناً لا شَكَّ فيهِ إذْ كَانَ الأَعْلى مِنَ
الأَسْفَلِ وَالأَسْفَلُ مِنَ الأَعْلى عَمَلُ العَجايِبِ
مِنْ واحِدٍ كَما كَانَتْ الأَشيَاءُ كُلُّها مِنْ واحِدٍ
وَأَبوهُ الشَّمْسُ وَأُمُّهُ القَمَرُ حَمَلَتْهُ الأَرْضُ في
بَطْنِهَا وَغَذَّتْهُ الرِّيحُ في بَطْنِهَا نَارًا صارَتْ أَرْضاً
أَغذوا الأَرْضَ مِنَ اللَطيف بِقُوَّةِ القُوى يَصْعَدُ
مِنَ الأَرْضِ إلى السماءِ فَيَكونُ مُسَلَّطاً عَلى
الأَعْلى والأَسْفَلِ

Truly, there is no doubt in it. Thus it was, the highest is from the lowest and the lowest from the highest, The working of wonders is from the one, just as all things come from the one. Its father is the Sun. Its mother is the Moon. The earth carries it in her belly. And the wind nourishes it in her belly, As Fire becoming Earth. Nourish the Earth with the subtle, through the power of powers, and it will ascend from the Earth to the Heaven and become one given authority over the highest and the lowest. *Emerald Tablet. Jābir ibn Hayyān. Kitāb Usṭuqus al-Uss. Book of the Foundation of the Elements.*

He makes explicit this link between things in the case of the seven planets and the seven metals.

♄ ♃ ♂ ☉

God of glory, by means of flowing in the seven planets, placed the seven metals in the bowels of the earth. Lead is placed by Saturn and because lead has the properties of Saturn, for that reason, lead is called Saturn. Tin is placed by Jupiter and because tin has the properties of Jupiter it is named Jupiter. Iron is placed by Mars and because iron has the properties of Mars we call it Mars. By the Sun, which is a more noble thing of all planets, because gold has the property of the Sun, for that reason we therefore call it the Sun.[152]

2.9 ml ethanol mp 292°C, potassium acetate 1gr.

And Rupescissa, continues like this, explaining the links between the seven planets and seven metals and suggesting a

151 Rupescissa. *DQE.* 58–59.

152 Rupescissa. *DQE.* 50–51.

cause and effect with the seven planets generating the seven metals. The metal is placed in the Earth by the planets. There is a generative link between the two with the planet placing or causing their own properties in the metals.

> ***The entire soul, both in us and in the universe, dwells in any member but most of all in the heart and in the Sun.***[153]

"Since this Quintessence or Spiritual Water is similar to Heaven, it is reasonable to put it between the Constellations and the Planets in order to adorn it with various influences and virtues." So writes Jean Brouaut, explaining this idea in his *Traite de l'Eau de Vie ou Anatomie Théorique et Pratique du Vin* (1646):

> ***...as the first Maker of the world creates the Heaven then, he adorns it with Celestial fires that we call Planets, for being signs and conductors of the times and the seasons, so we, after having made ours, that is to say, our Aqua Vitae made perfect, we must enrich it by its Planets and by other Constellations in order to influence and to irradiate the human Body so that, by the virtue of the said Planets, conservation would be attracted.***
> ***But by which Planets will we adorn it? The Heaven receives some of all types, so does this Celestial Water [...]***
> ***Since the Sun is the first among these, we must also assign first place to it in this. This Sun is the Gold that is the King of the metals and the most excellent Body; truly it would be the most perfect to us in the world.***[154]

The craftsman (I mean the sun) binds heaven to earth, sending essence below and raising matter above. *Corpus Hermeticum. XVI.5.*

The placement of the Sun in the Heavens creates an *aurum potabile,* a drinkable, liquid essence of gold. According to alchemical and medical theory of the time, gold possesses very potent qualities that touch the very heart of a person and was

153 Ficino. *Three Books.* 257.
154 Jean Brouaut. *Traité de l'Eau de Vie ou Anatomie Théorique et Pratique du Vin.* (Paris, 1646) 95.

used to treat illnesses like melancholia, heart pains, and eye disorders, to name a few. The challenge was to impart gold's virtues into a consumable form. So, how is this "Sun on Earth" placed into "our Heaven?" Once again, we find that Rupescissa has adapted the process from that used with wine. In *Liber de Vinis* (ca 1310), a work generally attributed to Arnald of Villanova (1240–1311), there are recipes for wine infusions similar to Dioscorides, and we find one for what is essentially an aurum potabile.

> **Wine of extinguished gold.** ***This wine has great property in many conditions. It is made when gold foil is extinguished four or five times in good wine and is left to clarify, then is carefully strained and saved.***
>
> ***It has indeed the power to strengthen the heart. It dries all excess away from the blood, the substance of the heart, and the spirit. It illuminates by its clarity, it strengthens by its solidity, it tempers by its temperament. By its heaviness, it inclines the excess to the expulsive parts of the body and to preserve the blood, to purify it of the corruption of the mixables. Youth is preserved and it causes the virtues of the minerals to abide in the operations and the tempering of those virtues.***[155]

Color of colloidal gold is dependent on particle size
Blue/violet – over 110 (nm)
Red – 15 to 90 (nm)
Orange – under 20 (nm)

Where Villanova uses wine, Rupescissa uses aqua ardens and the quintessence to draw out the virtues of gold.

> ***Take the gold of God cleansed by cementation, if you are able to have such gold or, if you are very poor, take the finest assayed florins of Florence. Make thin plates of them, put them to the fire and heat these on an iron plate, it is heated as iron is heated. Have near you a glazed-earth vessel filled***

155 Arnald Villanova. *Liber de Vinis.* (ca 1310). The process effectively transfers the potencies virtues of gold and other metals and minerals and in so doing also tempers or balances the virtues or potencies. Water of Iron, as described by al-Khawarizmī in *Key of the Sciences*, is made in a similar way, by taking heated iron and extinguishing it in water. Where Islamic medicine uses water, Villanova uses wine and Rupescissa uses Aqua ardens.

with the purest aqua ardens, and throw the fiery plates of gold into the aqua ardens.

And if you have a fire, extinguish it right away so that the water is not laid waste. Beware that no iron touches the water, but from a distance, throw the gold plates into it. And do this fifty times or more, because the more often the better it will be.

Note what I said to you this way, and if you see the aqua ardens decrease change it and take another and after that another. Put all the extinguishing water together. And I know for certain that God has created a kind of power in aqua ardens which draws out from the heated gold all the virtues of gold and incorporates in itself and retains the rays, light, color, and quality of incorruptibility, durability, solidity, and all the properties of the heavenly Sun. Then you mix the aqua ardens so* Solified *or aurified with the quintessence. And do not dare extinguish the plates of gold in the quintessence, because it will be lost.[156]

And for those Evangelical men who,

...if they do not have aqua ardens, in a good white wine, neither too light, nor too gross, but delectably the best, fragrant, flavorful, and gracious, because wine has a nature to receive in itself the influences and properties of

According to Gentile (da Fulgno. *Contra pestilentiam.* 1515) ... This is the method: Take one ounce of gold, two ounces of quicksilver, blend at the same time, mixing until such time as the gold dissolves. Then place in an alembic with a slow fire, and only the quicksilver will exit the alembic and add 47 ounces of *aqua buglossae*. Put into a glass alembic well stopped and make it undergo continuous fire for three days and nights,... you will find a little of the water consumed and the gold is liquefied. And this is *aurum potabile* most cordial and digestible. *Marsilio Ficino Epidemiarum Antidotus. Latin: Opera Omnia I; Bale 1576 p593.*

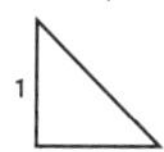

In dissolving all things, the cosmos renews them, and when things have been dissolved in this way, the cosmos (like life's good farmer) offers them renewal through the same process of change that moves the cosmos. *Corpus Hermeticum IX.6.*

The Tincture of Gold or Drinkable Gold of Mademoiselle Grimaldi: Take a *demi-gros* of the purest gold, dissolve in two ounces of aqua regia; pour on this solution, whose color will be of a beautiful yellow, one ounce of essential oil of rosemary. Mix the two liquors well together; leave the whole to rest. Soon after you will see the oil, tinted a hue of a beautiful yellow color, float on top the aqua regia which will have lost all its color. Separate your two liquors one from the other, by means of a funnel, by the end of which you will let run out all the aqua regia, & that you will stop with the finger, at once that oil will be ready to pass. Receive this oil in a flask, & mix it with five times its weight of rectified spirit of wine. Stop your flask with a wet bladder; put the mixture in digestion in the sand bath for one month. At the end of this time it will have taken a color crimson & a gracious flavor, but a little bitter & astringent. *Pierre Macquer's Dictionnaire de Chymie.*

156 Rupescissa. *DQE.* 52–53.

gold. And after you have finished your work at will, know for certain that the good florins are as before, or nearly so, noble and beautiful. Use therefore, the gilded wine or golden water, in order that you may live happy and healthy, and also in order to grow young.[157]

The quintessence is the means by which creation is preserved and maintained, and through which things connect with and influence each other. "Just as the power of our soul is brought to bear on our members through spirit, so the force of the World-soul is spread under the World-soul through all things through the quintessence."[158] The quintessence not only maintains the macrocosm but the microcosm as well. And if it is absorbed into the body, its health, vitality and vigor would be maintained. Rupescissa states that "the Most High created a quintessence not only in aqua ardens, but also in all things marvelous, enduring, having the virtue of the heavens."[159] The quintessence is in everything but in some things it is more pure and abundant and more easily absorbed as Ficino notes in his *Three Books on Life*:

This quintessence can be ingested by us more and more if a person knows how best to separate it, mixed in as it is with other elements or at least how to use those things often which are filled with it, especially in pure form. Such things are: choice wine, sugar, myrobalans and things which smell most sweet and which shine...whitest sugar, especially if you add to it gold and the odor of cinnamon and roses.[160]

Make when the Celestials descend into the Earth. Use when they rise from the Earth.

Ficino gives a wide range of recipes to maintain health and youth. They have both a material force derived from the elements of the world around us, and a more poetic or inner force arising from the web-like entanglement of objects and subjects. Here is his preparation to counteract melancholy.

157 Rupescissa. *DQE.* 54.
158 Ficino. *Three Books.* 257.
159 Rupescissa. *DQE.* 36.
160 Ficino. *Three Books.* 247.

Here is how you will have the gold almost potabile, I would say. Gather the flowers of borage, bugloss, and the Melissa which we call 'citraria,' and when the Moon enters Leo, Aries or Sagittarius and aspects the Sun or Jupiter, cook it with the whitest sugar dissolved in rose-water and carefully add three gold leaves per ounce. Take it on an empty stomach with a golden wine.[161]

Borage - *Borago officinalis*
Bugloss - possibly Viper's Bugloss - *Echium vulgare*
Melissa -Lemon balm - *Melissa officinalis*

For Marsilio Ficino these alchemical preparations are a way to balance the elements, and to harmonize the microcosm with the macrocosm – to make those channels conscious and the virtues accessible resulting in improved health, longevity, and vitality. He uses alchemical preparations to aid in the assimilation of virtues symbolized by the planets and so raise the "soul" step by step up the ladder of ascent. Dante describes a similar ascent in his *La Commedia Divina*. Ficino, in his *Commentary on Plato's Symposium* explains the meditative aspect of this ascent.

Now to the divine part of us are akin the motions, thoughts and revolutions of the whole universe. These everyman should follow, restoring the revolutions in our highest part that are corrupted by our wanderings about generation. *Iamblichus. The Exhortation to Philosophy.p39*

If any man then has an incorporeal eye, let him go forth from the body to behold the Beautiful, let him fly up and float aloft, not seeking to see shape or colour, but rather that by which these things are made, that which is quiet and calm, stable and changeless, ... that which is one, that which issues from itself and is contained in itself, that which is like nothing but itself. *Hermetica Fragmenta. 25. p543.*

Do you want to see the beauty of the Soul also? Take away from Corporeal beauty the weight of matter itself but the limitations of place; leave the rest. Now you have the beauty of the Soul. Do you want to see the beauty of the Angel as well? Take away, please, not only the spaces of place, but also the progression of time; keep the manifold composition; immediately you will find it. Do you want to see the beauty of God? Take away, in addition, that manifold composition of forms; leave utterly simple form; immediately you have reached the beauty of God.[162]

One thousand years earlier, we find in Alexandrian alchemy the implied use of tinctures as a support for meditation as in Zosimos's advice to Theosebia, his mystical sister:

161 Ficino. *Three Books.* 196.
162 Marsilio Ficino. *Commentary on Plato's Symposium On Love.* Trans. with and Introduction and notes. Sears Jayne. (Dallas: Spring Publications, 1985) 139.

Ignorance, grief, incontinence, lust, injustice, greed, deceit, envy, treachery, anger, recklessness, malice. *Corpus Hermeticum XIII.7.*

Rest your body, calm your passions, resist desire, pleasure, anger, sorrow, and the twelve fatalities of death. In thus conducting yourself you will call to yourself the divine being, and the divine being will come to you, he who is everywhere and nowhere.
[...]
By operating in this way you will obtain the proper, authentic, and natural tinctures. Make these things until you become perfect in your soul. But, when you recognize that you have arrived at perfection, then beware the intervention of the natural elements of the material: descending toward the Shepard, and plunging into meditation, ascend to your origin.[163]

Leave the senses of the body idle, and the birth of divinity will begin. Cleanse yourself of the irrational torments of matter. *Corpus Hermeticum. XIII.7.*

The Byzantine philosopher, alchemist, Stephanos of Alexandria takes this neo-Platonic vision and connects it to Alexandrian alchemy echoing Plato's description of the soul's journey from sensible, to abstract, to authentic beauty. He adds here a warning to the practitioner not to become mesmerized by the physical transformations or spiritual transformations and to cut through each stage.

Rise from what is below up to the transcendent, and the more it climbs the more language falters and when it has passed up and beyond the ascent, it will turn silent completely. *Dionysus the Aeropagite Mystical Theology p 139.*

From the objects of sense perception pass over now to those sights which are perceived by the mind. Behold the great order and immaterial splendor of the heavenly bodies. When thou hast seen the beauties of these, lift up thy mind beyond and noting the resplendent glory and great joy of angels do not here after be led astray with respect to the material transformation of this earthly substance, of that which is sought after with the hand and revealed by the philosophy of making gold.

But elevate thy whole mind towards the things on high. Sending its flight toward the luminous forms of the uppermost beings behold with intelligent eyes their innumerable and inconceivable beauties and directing the gaze toward that light which is

163 Zosimus. *First Book of the Final Reckoning* in Berthelot, Vol 2. 235–36.

above every other light admire all the works that have been placed in the universe.

[...]

Reflect with deliberation upon death. Having utterly killed the body, and having also besides denied thy soul, glorify and praise the universal King of all and Lord of Glory with hymns that are never silent. Stand in awe of His almighty power with trembling and fear. Reflect upon His most excellent goodness and how all things have been brought about by means of His unspeakable wisdom. Tongue and mind are confuted for they have not strength to bear up or wholly to search out and declare the works of the Omnipotent.[164]

Cutting through them all, it will fly to the utmost body. But if you wish to break through the universe itself and look upon the things outside (if, indeed, there is anything outside the cosmos), it is within your power. *Corpus Hermeticum XI.19*

And those more courageous cut even this.

here,
at the limit
an ocean without bounds
amongst the cinders
i
sat
and all
around
spring
surged green ...

164 Stephanos of Alexandria. *On The Great and Sacred Art of Making Gold.* (C.A. Browne Papers Mss Col 418 NYCPL.)

BUT HOW IS THIS TO BE ACCOMPLISHED?

CUT AWAY EVERYTHING.

Plotinus. Ennead V.3.17.

Alchemy starts with the body, with the material, in the here and now, and it penetrates to the border, the event horizon of being. It is by and through matter that the meditation on creation lies. The challenge is to find the balance in the work to create, while not getting over involved in what Stephanos of Alexandria refers to as a "strange display of the marvelous."[165] These "displays" are manifestations, provoked or created through alchemy to demonstrate the underlying material and non-material structure and flow of creation. These displays, while perhaps reflecting an inner state or station and therefore are positive phenomena, may distract from the "ascent of the soul" – the central work of alchemy, in that they become the goal instead.

The highest purpose of the hieratic art is to ascend to the one, which is supreme master of the whole of multiplicity *Iamblichus. De Mysteriis V:22*

Alchemical practice involves the material and the non-material and the union of the two. It is the union of creative practice and its inner creative state, and the ascent practice whatever form it may take. In other words, there is an aspect concerned with matter and technique and another aspect concerned primarily with the "ascent of the soul." It is an artificial distinction, but a temporary and necessary one to make clear the importance of the balance between these two axes of alchemy.

The range of this thinking extends from on high all the way down to conclusions in the sense world, where it touches on nature and cooperates with natural science in establishing many of its propositions, just as it rises up from below and nearly joins intellect in apprehending primary principles. *Proclus A Commentary on the First Book of Euclid's Elements p17.*

These two aspects can be thought of as intersecting horizontal and vertical lines. By the horizontal I mean to designate the concern with the material world and its manipulation, the realm of technology/sorcery. Technology and magic are equated in that their concern is with the manipulation of matter towards, more often than not, a material or ego-gratifying end. This is opposed to the vertical concern with the manipulation of the material world for wisdom/gnosis and its ideas and goals of ascent, transcendence, union with the divine, or enlightenment.

Any sufficiently advanced technology is indistinguishable from magic. *Arthur C. Clarke. Profiles of the Future. (New York: Harper and Row, 1973) 21.*

We can use the material world to gain control over aspects of the material world either to better the world and our lives in it, or for greed. We can as well use matter for the vertical ascent of gnosis – wisdom, the ascent from sensible to abstract to authentic beauty.

Now call up all your confidence, you need a guide no longer; strain and see. *Plotinus Enneads. I.6.9.*

165 Stephanos of Alexandria. *On The Great and Sacred Art of Making Gold.* (C.A. Browne Papers Mss Col 418 NYCPL.)

Thus even as they create all things by images, so also they signify them in the same way by agreed-upon signs; and perhaps they even awaken our understanding, by the same impulse to a greater acuteness. *Iamblichus. On The Mysteries. p157*

Since it was proper not even for terrestrial things to be utterly deprived of participation in the divine, earth also has received from it a share in divinity, such as is sufficient for it to be able to receive the gods. *Iamblichus. On the mysteries. P267 (V.23.223)*

> ***Just as lovers systematically leave behind what is fair to sensation and attain the one true source of all that is fair and intelligible, in the same way priests – observing how all things are in all from the sympathy that all visible things have for one another and for the invisible powers – have also framed their priestly knowledge. For they were amazed to see the last in the first and the very first in the last; in heaven they saw earthly things acting causally and in a heavenly manner, in the earth heavenly things in an earthly manner.***[166]

In this we can recognize the Platonic aspect, but we can also see a reference to the *Emerald Tablet* in that each arises with the other, Earth and Heaven, Above and Below and the horizontal aspect of the Sun and Moon. It is this insight into how things come to be that is the power behind the creative act in the hieratic art. And like all art, the composition comes from a deep understanding of *sympatheia* – the union and tension among the elements of composition, of poetry.

Seek out the channel of the soul, from where it descended in a certain order to serve the body; and seek how you will raise it up again to its order by combining action with sacred word... It perfects the soul by means of material powers – that is by means of symbols. *Chaldean Oracle. Fragment 110*

> ***The wise man is he who knows how all things are bound together in this world; he makes one thing come to him through the intermediary of another thing; with the assistance of the present objects he extends his power over the most distant objects; he works by means of words, figures and material substances.***[167]

These compositions, poems, and constructions and the relationships and identities that arise from them, are the essence of the hieratic art – the clustering of objects to form a "psychic" whole, a talisman, the intent of which was spiritual – union with the divine. This whole, as it arises into its unity, is infused with the "divine" or aspects of the divine, as symbolized by the planets, metals, etc. This is done on an inner level by visualizing an object and then separating out its mass,

166 Proclus. *On The Priestly Art According To The Greeks*. Trans Brian Copenhaver in Merkel and Debus *Hermeticism and the Renaissance*. (Cambridge: Cambridge UP, 1992) 103 – 105.

167 Synesios. *On Dreams by Saint Synesios*. (Philadelphia, 1888) 4.

its substance, but still allowing it to exist as the idea or image whose form is outlined in light.

As the composition is made, this "pure receptacle" is then filled. Here Plotinus (204–270 CE) speaks of the cosmos but any created object can be used.[168] There is the making and the filling, not as separate stages but as interdependent actions, giving rise to the final result.

For geometry is the knowledge of the eternally existent." "Then, my good friend, it would tend to draw the soul to truth, and would be productive of a philosophic attitude of mind, directing upward the faculties that now wrongly are turned earthward. *Plato. Republic [527b]*

Let us, then, make a mental picture of our universe: each member shall remain what it is, distinctly apart; yet all is to form, as far as possible, a complete unity so that whatever comes into view shall show as if it were the surface of the orb over all, bringing immediately with it the vision, on the one plane, of the sun and of all the stars with earth and sea and all living things as if exhibited upon a transparent globe.

In the moment when you have nothing to say about it, you will see it, for the knowledge of it is divine silence and suppression of all the senses. *Corpus Hermeticum X.5*

Bring this vision actually before your sight, so that there shall be in your mind the gleaming representation of a sphere, a picture holding sprung, themselves, of that universe and repose or some at rest, some in motion. Keep this sphere before you, and from it imagine another, a sphere stripped of magnitude and of spatial differences; cast out your inborn sense of Matter, taking care not merely to attenuate it: call on God, maker of the sphere whose image you now hold, and pray Him to enter. And may He come bringing His own Universe with all the Gods that dwell in it — He who is the one God and all the gods, where each is all, blending into a unity, distinct in powers but all one god in virtue of that one divine power of many facets.

Plotinus Vth Ennead, Eight Tractate, 9.

I have seen! Language is not able to reveal this. For the entire eighth, my son, and the souls that are in it, and the angels, sing a hymn in silence. *Nag Hammadi Library. Discourse on the Eight and Ninth (VI,6.58. 16–21)*

168 *Cosmos* comes from the Greek kosmos meaning arrangement. The chapter in Ficino's *Three Books on Life*, "How to Construct a Figure of the Universe" gives instruction on constructing a physical model for contemplation based on planetary relationships in terms of material and time. Ficino. *Three Books*. 343.

In making the recepticle we return again to *sympatheia*, which holds that potency and balance can be made manifest. Proclus explains,

For all things are interwoven and separate afresh, and all things are mingled and all things combine, all things are mixed and all unmixed, all things are moistened and all things dried and all things flower and blossom in the altar shaped like a bowl. For each, it is by method, by measure and weight of the 4 elements, that the interlacing and dissociation of all is accomplished. No bond can be made without method. It is a natural method, breathing in and breathing out, keeping the arrangements of the method, increasing or decreasing them. When all things, in a word, come to harmony by division and union, without the methods being neglected in any way, the nature is transformed. *Zosimos. On Virtue Lesson 2*

But as of statues established by telestic art, some things pertaining to them are manifest, but others are inwardly concealed, being symbolical of the presence of the gods, and which are only known to the mystic artists themselves, after the same manner, the world being a statue of the intelligible. *Proclus. The Commentaries of Proclus on the Timaeus of Plato. Trans. Thomas Taylor p175*

> ***They used mixing because they saw that each unmixed thing possesses some property of the god but is not enough to call that god forth. Therefore, by mixing many things they unified the aforementioned influences and made a unity generated from all of them similar to the whole that is prior to them all. And they often devised composite statues and fumigations, having blended separate signs together into one and having made artificially something embraced essentially by the divine through unification of many powers,...***[169]

Alchemy is, in a very real sense, a "hieratic art." All the pieces invoke the whole, creating a "living" entity, but here, instead of awakening the divine within through the art of animating statues, a living "medicine" is brought forth – an elixir of the heart. An elixir that makes whole, it completes, it perfects and creates a result, and this result is able to effect change. It engages both axes using the material as the basis, or prop, for ascent. By engaging in action, in performing a material act the hidden geometries, proportions common to all creation are awakened in the soul. This kind of unity of action manifests in alchemical results that can in turn affect the world and its inhabitants. Here, Marsilio Ficino shows how things come together:

> ***Certainly you know that the lower nature cannot hold all the forces of the higher nature in one subject; and, therefore, that these forces are dispersed in our world through many natures; and that they can be collected more easily through medical procedures and the like than through images.***[170]

169 Merkel and Debus. 103 – 105. Proclus. "On The Priestly Art According To The Greeks." Trans Brian. Copenhaver

170 Ficino. *Three Books*. 307 -309. Although Ficino does state images are useful and that gems and metals are "apt materials for capturing and holding celestial things."

This is a very intriguing statement mostly due to the use of his words "medical procedures" and "images." By medical procedures, he is referring to the composition of medicines. For example, the use of alchemical procedures in unifying the fixed and the volatile as discussed earlier. It isn't that the use of images, visual talismans for example, couldn't unify these forces, but it is easier with matter through the known methods of composition of medicinal powders. Equally important was Ficino's understanding that images were a potential entry point for demonic forces and that their use should be approached, if at all, with great caution. Indeed, when one tries to locate the source of the image's power, we find ourselves on shifting ground in searching for the source of its meaning. This shifting quality is a worrisome one for those of limited scope. For others this shifting ground is another entry point to a deeper understanding of alchemy.

The world is the statue of the intelligible gods;... But it is a statue in motion, and full of life, and deity; fashioned from all things within itself; preserving all things. *Procl Comm. Parmen. p471*

Perhaps hammering and heating alone brings out the power latent in the material, if it is done at the right time. It is a good idea to use the right time in making up medicines. *Ficino. Three Books. 343.*

As is clear from Ficino and others, in making these talismans or results, not only the material arrangements are considered, but the arrangement in time and space as well. That is, the positions and movements of the Sun, Moon, and planets as they mark time along the arc of infinity. And, in considering these movements, do so, not just in a material sense of the forces of gravity, electromagnetism, etc., but also in the relationships of the Earth, sky, movements, and the meaning that arises from their interplay. This relationship is a poetic one, co-emerging out of myth, poetry, art, the history of human evolution and culture.

God makes eternity; eternity makes the cosmos; the cosmos makes time; time makes becoming. *Corpus Hermeticum XI.2*

Your fire must be like the heat of the sun. At the time the matter is raised it is extremely hot. That is, when the Dog rises up in the East. Those days are suitable for the pounding, the transformation and the washing. *Zosimos. Muṣḥaf as-Ṣuwar. The Book of Pictures. p494*

Time has two aspects: *Kronos* and *Kairos*. *Kronos* is concerned with linear time based on orbits, rotations, and now vibrations of matter. This is the realm of astronomy, astrology, chronometry etc. Mythically, it's the image of the Grim Reaper. *Kairos* means the "exact or critical time, season, opportunity,"[171] it is also the word for weather. It has the sense of something impermanent, sudden and passing. It is "the appointed time in the purpose of God."[172] It is the time when God acts. To the ancient

Facing West
eye to eye...
Earth rises
to embrace...

171 Καιρος. Henry George Liddell, Robert Scott. *A Greek-English Lexicon.*

172 Richardson and Bowden. *The Westminster Dictionary of Christian Theology.* (Philadelphia: Westminster, 1983) 316.

Oh nature, whatever your seasons bear is fruit for me; all things from you, all things in you, all things into you. *Marcus Aurelius Meditations 4.23*

Greeks, *Kairos* is the god of "the fleeting moment." The adage "strike while the iron is hot," expresses *Kairos* perfectly. It is the point, the infinitesimal point that opens onto infinite possibilities, onto eternity[173] itself. I have found, through my work, that alchemical time is best described by *Kairos*, that moment when an action is effective or possible.

In every action there is nothing better than the right time. *Iamblichus. On the Pythagorean way of Life. p73*

All things are from him and through him and into him. *Romans 11:36*

Seal your words with silence, and your silence with kairos. *Plotinus. (Solon 1.63.16)*

Kronos as expressed through astrology is the symbolic system of time as it intersects with humanity. As measured time it is the intersection of the arcs of space and the alternations of the heart. By the Sun we find the day, with the heart, the seconds.[174] There are other arrangements based less on position and more on sympathetic relationships between a particular planet and a particular time of day.[175] In Alexandrian alchemy, this moment, the ideal time to start the work, is the Egyptian Month of Pharmouthi.[176] Iamblichus also notes that the ideal time and the reason for beginning work is in the "... spring, since this is just when the whole world receives from the gods the power of generating all creation."[177] From the dead of winter arise the buds of spring. What better time to start anything than to ride the tidal surge of spring's creative energies? The above comes from the below and the below comes from the above. In early alchemy, it seems to be about the relation between planets, not strictly from an astrological point of view, as we understand it today but more with an emphasis on sympatheia. For example, in the work of Stephanos of Alexandria, we see a more symbolic use of the planets to reflect the actual practical work. Again in using the word "symbolic," I don't mean that it stands for, or points to, something, but that it is an expression, an aspect, of the same process – or they are the same expression in different media.

(5) Again the star of Venus, allotted to the eastern dawn, ushers in the rays of the Sun. Again the star of Mercury is discovered towards those which fol-

173 Don't think of eternity as endless time. It is not an infinity of minutes. The cosmos generates time, abstract the cosmos and time evaporates. Behold eternity.

174 This is another link between the Sun and the heart.

175 See Cotnoir. *Alchemy*. 41–47. Also Cotnoir. *On Alchemy and the Timing of Things*. (New York: Khepri Press, 2017) 12–13.

176 Depending on the calendar it is roughly March 27 – April 26.

177 Iamblichus. *Iamblichus, De Mysteriis*. (Atlanta: Society of Biblical Literature, 2003) 49.

low beneath the rays of the Sun. Again the star of Saturn gleams dimly forth from the deep recess of his height. Again the star of Mars completes his fiery course. Among them the Moon advances attired like a bride; she takes on the nine changes of her phases and by means of her the blended mixture is made perfect.

Remember that in the kerotakis work, the tetrasoma; iron, tin, copper, and lead are fused and worked. This action is "mirrored" both in the microcosm and macrocosm. Here the composition of the tetrasoma is shown in the movements of the planets and relates to the appearances and disappearances of metals and colors. "By means of her the blended mixture is made perfect," "her" meaning the Moon, meaning silver; "made perfect" meaning here on Earth, meaning here in the Heavens. All are simultaneously true.

Morienus to Khālid:

Now I will explain further to you about this, the whole good of which consists in seeking the joining and concordance of bodies which are shattered and then brought together again and which are so purified and treated as to appear distinctly by the power of fire.[178]

and so the great work is engaged.

178 Morienus. 1974. 35.

OPUS MAGNUM

A THOUGHT EXPERIMENT

Morienus replied: "Before I explain them to you, I will bring before you the things called by these names, that you may see them, as well as work with them in your presence."

PART I

ALCHEMICAL TRANSMUTATION BY THE PHYSICAL MEANS AVAILABLE

put in front of yourself the material necessary for the work
        put aside all that you think you know
and
        approach the material as directly as possible
                examine it all
        ask
how do you take what is before you
and turn it
        into the philosopher's stone
or at least
gold

PART II

THE SQUARING OF THE CIRCLE

the squaring of the circle is not possible
        (using only compass and straight edge)
go beyond the given tools
                straight edge
                and compass
        will not
                suffice
Like the monk says,
        "the only thing that is
missing comes
        from you
for you are its mine"

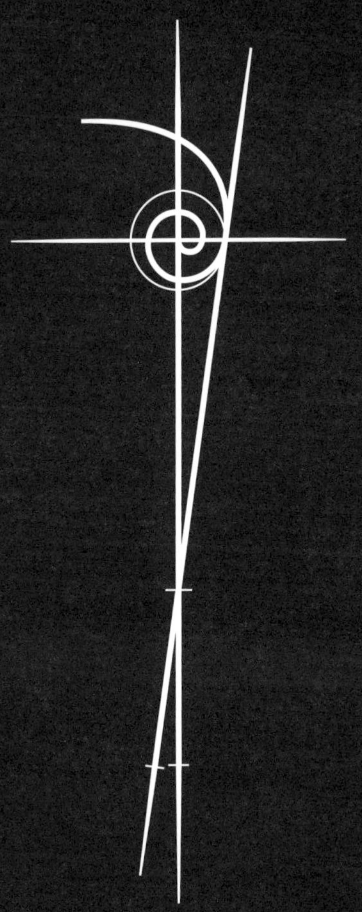

...saying these things,
i went to sleep...

EMERALD TABLET

...with this truth, entangled in words, inscribed...
The higher is from the lower.
The lower is from the higher.

The working of wonders comes from the one,
as all things originate together from one and the same,
by the same governance.

Whose father is the Sun, but whose mother, the Moon.
The wind lifts it up in its own body,
the earth becomes sweeter.

You therefore, sons of deceptions,
workers of wonders,
of perfect discretion,

if it should become earth, lead it out of fire
which surpasses all grossness and what is ponderous,
draw it forth expansively and prudently and by the hard work of wisdom.

From the earth, it will rise to the heaven,
it will slip down from heaven to earth,
containing the force and potential of the higher and lower things.

Therefore from out of the same thing all obscurity is illuminated.
Namely, whose power transcends whatever is subtle and enters
whole into gross matter.

This operation indeed, has its being according to the composition
of the greater world.
Hermes Philosopher calls this namely, three-fold wisdom, or, three-
fold knowledge.

TABULA SMARAGDINA

hac verborum intricata veritate descriptam...
Superiora de inferioribus,
inferiora de superioribus.

Prodigiorum operatio ex uno,
quemadmodum omnia ex uno eodemque ducunt originem una
eademque consilii administratione.

Cujus pater Sol, mater vero Luna.
Eam ventus in corpore suo extollit,
terra fit dulcior.

Vos ergo praestigiorum filii,
prodigiorum opifices,
discretione perfecti,

Si terra fiat, eam ex igne subtili,
qui omnem grossitudinem et quod hebes est antecellit,
spaciosus et prudentia et sapientiae industria educite.

A terra ad caelum conscendet,
a caelo ad terram dilabitur,
superiorum et inferiorum vim continens atque potentiam.

Unde omnis ex eodem illuminatur obscuritas.
Cujus videlicet potentia quicquid subtilis est
transcendit et rem grossam totum ingreditur.

Quae quidem operatio secundum majoris mundi compositionem
habet subsistere.

Quod videlicet Hermes philosophus triplicem sapientiam vel triplicem
scientiam appellat.

NEITHER TALKING NOR CONCEALING
BUT GIVING INDICATIONS BY SIGNS